N £8·50

THE BERBERS

THE BERBERS
Their Social and Political Organisation

ROBERT MONTAGNE

Translated and with an Introduction by
DAVID SEDDON
Lecturer in African Anthropology,
School of Oriental and African Studies,
University of London

With a Preface by
ERNEST GELLNER

FRANK CASS : LONDON

First published in 1931 by
la Société de l'Afrique Française
as *La Vie Sociale et la Vie Politique des Berbères*

© 1931 Robert Montagne

This translation first published 1973 in Great Britain by
FRANK CASS AND COMPANY LIMITED
67 Great Russell Street, London WC1B 3BT, England

and in United States of America by
FRANK CASS AND COMPANY LIMITED
c/o International Scholarly Book Services, Inc.
P.O. Box 4347, Portland, Oregon 97208

Translation and Introduction copyright © 1973 David Seddon

ISBN 0 7146 2968 5

Library of Congress Catalog Card No. 72-92972

Printed in Great Britain by
T. & A. CONSTABLE LTD, Edinburgh

Contents

List of Maps

Preface

France entered the North African world in 1830. Its overt political role there ended in 1962. The interpenetration of cultures and languages which resulted from the colonial conquest has not ended yet. No doubt a time will come when an intellectual balance sheet of this epoch comes to be drawn up.

When this is done, Robert Montagne's name will head the list of those Frenchmen who have made a study of Berber society. The brilliance of his ideas, the thoroughness and perceptiveness of his documentation, the range of his historical and comparative vision, and (a trait not always found in scholarly writing on North Africa) the simplicity and vigour of his style, all help to make plain that we have here a social thinker and observer of the very first rank, and one who deserves to be far better known outside the French-speaking world than he is at present.

It would be idle and pointless to pretend that he was not closely associated with French colonialism. No doubt he was a patriotic Frenchman, a naval officer seconded for research which, inevitably, combined ethnography and political intelligence. No doubt he was a man concerned with whether developments were or were not favourable to the influence, prosperity and power of France. It is hardly possible to attempt here an assessment of such values, but it would be absurd for anyone who holds such values to be suspect, to fail in consequence to appreciate the superb quality of Montagne's sociological observation and analysis. The two issues are independent. Though Montagne's sociology is illuminated by the context of his political involvement, its merit is quite independent of it, and should be appreciated even (or perhaps especially) by those who do not share his position.

His politically most committed book was also his last, *Revolution au Maroc* (1953). Its specific predictions were falsified within a couple of years—yet it remains, if one knows how to read it, a brilliant and insightful introduction to the Moroccan politics of the next decade and a half. In substance, it argued that the young radical modernist nationalists could not succeed in their aims, for they ignored the old Morocco which he knew so well. In the event, they did, in alliance with the monarchy, succeed in dismantling the French Protectorate. But Montagne's analysis happens to explain the process by which the monarchy then in turn neutralised and defeated the radicals. We sociologists may sometimes succeed in discerning a general structure, but we should be well advised not to be too specific in drawing up a list of dramatis personae. Montagne's analysis continued to be valid, at any rate up to the abortive coup of July 1971. It was merely necessary to read 'Monarchy' for 'Protectorate'.

But this book, fascinating though it is, is not the most important point of intersection of Montagne's scholarly and political concerns. For that we must look to the very heart of his work, to his central ideas on the political sociology of the Berbers. In this area, he put forward two main theses: one, that the principal agency of the maintenance of order in the Berber anarchic milieu was the moiety, the *leff* or *soff*; and secondly, that Berber society tends to oscillate between democratic/oligarchic tribal republics, and ephemeral personal tyrannies. I believe the first of these ideas to be but a half-truth (correct in its stress on balance and opposition as the mechanism of stability, but wrong in its stress on binary organisation), whereas the second one seems to me wholly correct. But what is fascinating is the way in which this valid perception sprang from a political predicament. French policy in Morocco was, in effect, an indirect rule policy—but which were the local elites or institutions that were to be employed? In the event, two quite different methods were followed. On the one hand, there was the *politique des grands caids*, the use of the big robber barons of the Western High Atlas; and on the other, the underwriting of tribal customary law, and hence of the egalitarian tribal assembly and organisation which that law presupposed. Roughly speaking, the first policy was applied in the South, and the second in Central Morocco. Where the two regions met, the result could be anomalous.

It is fair to suspect that it was this policy dilemma which led Montagne to his theory of oscillation, which he then proceeded to illustrate brilliantly from historical as well as ethnographic material. As David Seddon observes, he was under no obligation, such as British social anthropologists sometimes felt at the time, to ignore history in order to display his liberation from *a priori* evolutionist schemata.

The fact that, through him, we can understand French involvement in Morocco, does not diminish the extent to which he also brilliantly illuminates his avowed and manifest subject, Berber society, and the wider topic of the symbiosis of tribal societies with urban-based, centralised governments and literate civilisations. The type of society in which politically autonomous segmentary tribes co-exist with a sophisticated world religion and its institutions, cannot really be assimilated to those favourite stereotypes, 'feudal' and 'oriental' or 'bureaucratic' societies. It deserves to be treated as at least one separate genus on its own. Anyone attempting to do so will find Montagne's work of outstanding value.

The present work presents his specific findings about the Berber world in an elegant and succinct form. It is an excellent introduction to his more detailed work, but it also stands on its own as a major contribution to the understanding of Islam and of Africa. Students of pre-industrial civilisations and of tribal societies alike, and of course anyone concerned with the Middle East or with Africa, must welcome the appearance of this translation.

ERNEST GELLNER

Notes on Translation and Transcription

The translation is based on Robert Montagne's 1947 MS., which includes a number of alterations and several additions to the earlier published text of 1931, as well as an entirely new 'conclusion' to the work as a whole. This latter was published in the memorial volume of *L'Afrique et l'Asie* referred to in my introduction.

The French text is admirably clear and straightforward, for the most part, and presents no particular problems. Several factors make it difficult, however, to utilise a wholly consistent method of transcription when translating a French text which has made use of its own versions of Arabic and Berber words. In general I have regarded the words of Arabic and Berber origin used in the French text as part of the French text and have merely converted them from French conventional transcription of Moroccan words to English forms (i.e. Tetuan instead of Tetouan; Wezzan instead of Ouezzane, etc.). In such cases, where the words are not proper or place names, I have identified them as being of Arabic or Berber origin by placing them in italics on their first appearance; thereafter they appear in the English text (as in the French text) *as if* they were European words (i.e. amghars, qāids, etc.). A glossary of all such words is to be found on pp. 87-89. Where a word of Arabic or Berber origin is used in its proper form in the plural (i.e. *shorfa* instead of sherifs) I have placed it in italics whenever it appears.

The only exception to the above is the word marabout (normally *mrabit* in English transcription) and related words, which retain their French flavour; I have for instance coined the word maraboutic as an adjective from the noun marabout, although the latter could certainly also be translated as 'saint.'

The following equivalents denote particular consonants unfamiliar to the English ear:

  ' —ain —as in 'Abd el Krim.

gh—ghain—as in *Gharb*; pronounced as French 'r'.

kh—khāf —as in *makhzen*; pronounced as 'ch' in Scottish *loch*.

Editorial notes are indicated by raised numerals in the text, and appear at the end of each chapter. Notes appearing at the foot of the page are translated from the original text.

Introduction

Robert Montagne was born in Le Mans in western France on the 19th of January 1893. After his secondary education he entered naval college in 1911 and, while there, discovered that he was as much interested by philosophy and the new subject of sociology as by matters more closely connected with the sea. At the time he wrote:

> I hesitated for a long while between the 'école normale' and the 'école navale'; and finally chose the latter. In fact I never regretted it, although on looking back it was clearly a mistake, because the Navy managed to teach me a good deal nevertheless.

Between 1913 and 1914 Montagne sailed as a young cadet in the training ship *Jeanne d'Arc* as far afield as Karachi, and circumnavigated Africa. His interest in the social life of the peoples whose countries he visited, however briefly, is recorded in the very full diary that he kept throughout this period. Scarcely had he returned from this training voyage aboard the *Jeanne d'Arc* when the First World War broke out and he was posted as a junior officer aboard a small destroyer. Towards the end of the War, in 1918, he was transferred to the naval flying corps and there, on the basis of his invention of a new aiming device, was promoted to instructor.

After the War he remained in the 'Aéro-Navale' and was sent to Port-Lyautey on the Atlantic coast of Morocco, which had become a French Protectorate in 1912. Here he applied himself, in what little spare time he had, to learning Arabic and Berber, and began also to make contact with the local population around the naval base. As his linguistic competence increased he enlarged his knowledge of local customs and local social organisation. He carried out a number of minor investigations of a sociological nature, some of which were published and at least one of which came to the attention of the French Resident-General, Marshal Lyautey. Lyautey arranged to meet the young man and, impressed by his evident abilities, suggested that he join the team of young officers being formed at the Institut des Hautes Etudes Marocaines. Montagne was delighted and thus came, effectively, to leave the Navy, although he maintained his official connection with the service until 1940.

His new job gave Montagne the opportunity to deepen his knowledge of Arabic and his understanding of Muslim society; and, largely as a result of his somewhat unusual expertise, he was assigned an equally unusual task. He was to travel in the High Atlas wherever possible among the Berber-speaking tribes, and to gather information about their social and political organisation. This information, it was hoped, would facilitate the 'pacification' by the French of these mountain regions which had hitherto proved hostile and intractable. He also visited the Rif mountain regions of northern Morocco and, when the French became involved in 1924-1925 in the war between the Rif tribes under 'Abd el Krim and the Spanish[1] his knowledge of Berber social and political organisation was of considerable utility to the French forces. Indeed, he eventually played a significant part in bringing about the surrender of 'Abd el Krim to the French. The attempts of 'Abd el Krim to build a 'republic' or 'Berber state' in the Rif provided Montagne with a living example of the process of state formation among Berber tribes that he was later to take as one of the main themes for investigation and analysis.

After the defeat of 'Abd el Krim in 1927 Montagne returned to his studies and his explorations in the south of Morocco. During the next two years he travelled extensively and worked in the hills and mountains of southern Morocco; talking directly to the people themselves, either to local chiefs or to commoner informants, Montagne put his linguistic skills to good use and obtained a great deal of detailed, first-hand information of the sort that could not be found in the literary sources. Some of this information he published immediately in the *Archives de la Direction des Affaires Indigènes*, but the greater part of it provided him with the basis for his wide-ranging study of Berber society, published later as *Les Berbères et le Makhzen dans le Sud du Maroc*. In 1929-30 he completed his research and wrote his doctoral thesis—a study of the Berbers, both past and present, focused for the most part on the south of Morocco, but also incorporating material gathered himself in the field or else from the literature relating to other regions of Morocco and even of Algeria and Tunisia. He was not content during this period merely to investigate the situation in the country-side but also showed a lively interest in the problems associated with the ever-growing rural exodus and the associated development of an urban proletariat. Such interests are merely hinted at in his writings of the 1930's but they were to become of overriding concern to him some twenty years later.

In 1930 he was appointed Director of the Institut Français in Damascus and he took up residence there the same year. In Syria he continued his work as a sociologist in addition to his official duties: he collected Bedouin folk-tales and items of their material culture, and also made a detailed study of their mode of existence in the desert, which was published in 1946 as *La Civilisation du Désert*. At the same time he cultivated a deep personal interest in the general political evolution of the Arab world as a whole and in the direction of French policy in the Levant in particular.

He returned to France in 1932 to found the Centre des Hautes Etudes d'Administration Musulmane (C.H.E.A.M.), a teaching institution and centre for documentation relating to all aspects of administration in the Muslim countries under French rule. The C.H.E.A.M. remains an important centre for sociological, political and historical research-workers and scholars of all nationalities, even today. The first class of the new Centre—his 'first litter', as Montagne enjoyed calling it—graduated in the spring of 1937. The 'pupils' in this class, as in the thirteen which followed it, were men who had already gained some experience in their different fields in the overseas territories. They included administrators concerned with native affairs, other civil servants of various sorts, university teachers and research-workers, forestry experts, doctors, diplomats, bankers and missionaries.

Although based in Paris, Montagne found time to visit North Africa from time to time; in the winter of 1934-1935, for instance, he gave a course on the sociology of Islam at the University of Algiers, and also visited Tunisia. In the winter of 1936 he was in Algiers once again to teach at the University. On the outbreak of the Second World War in 1939 he was appointed to the general staff of General Nogues in Algeria, and there, together with an old friend and colleague from the Moroccan days, Lévi-Provençal, he ran the political bureau concerned with Middle Eastern affairs. After the fall of France and the formation of the Vichy government Montagne tried desperately to transfer the C.H.E.A.M. and its valuable archives out of harm's way to North Africa and, finally, with the assistance of General Weygand and his assistant M. de Witasse, he managed to establish the Centre in Algiers, and even to begin teaching there. At the same time he acted as official advisor on Middle Eastern, and more particularly on North African, affairs. When the Comité de la Libération created a Commissariat d'Etat aux Affairs Musulmanes in 1943 its director, General Catroux, chose Montagne as his right-hand man. Montagne also founded during this period the organisation that was later to become, under Lévi-Provençal and Colombe, L'Institut de l'Orient Contemporain, and laid down the bases for the development, after the War, of a number of organisations concerned with Islamic studies and the education of administrative officials in social studies.

After the liberation of France Montagne remained for a few months, supervising the return of the C.H.E.A.M. to Paris, and then returned himself to direct the Centre. The first class began in autumn 1945 and the Centre expanded rapidly after that date: a section concerned with Islam in Black Africa was opened in 1946, and an Asian section started the following year. Through his formal teaching and his informal influence, Montagne came to have a profound effect upon a whole generation of overseas administrators, bureaucrats, businessmen and others; and as the members of the 'zawia Montagne' (as it came to be called) took up their posts abroad once again, they remembered, and frequently obeyed, their teacher's injunction to study the peoples among whom they worked and whom, in some cases, they were required to administer, and to carry out, wherever possible, sociological investigations 'in the field'.

Despite all this administrative and educational work Montagne still found time to organise seminars and conferences, to make visits to Belgium, Holland, Great Britain and the United States, and to carry out research in Algeria and Morocco. At the end of 1947 he was formally attached to the Collège de France and in 1949 he was made Professor there. His heavy commitments in France were not too great to prevent him making a number of prolonged visits to North Africa and a couple of shorter ones to Nigeria and Cameroun.

Between 1949 and 1951 his interest in the question of labour migration from the rural areas of North Africa and the associated 'urbanisation' led him to carry out a number of investigations of this phenomenon in Morocco and Algeria. Much of this research appeared in 1951 with the publication of an important work on aspects of urbanisation under Montagne's editorship: *Naissance du Prolétariat Marocain*, but a certain amount remains unpublished (notably some investigations of the proletariat in the mining areas around Ujda, in north-east Morocco). He also made studies of labour migration in Algeria, and of migration from North Africa to France, which were published in article form between 1951 and 1953. This specific research interest did not blind him to the more general aspects of social, economic and political change that were to become ever more alarming to many Frenchmen over the next decade, and in 1952 his last book appeared. In this brilliant work, *Révolution au Maroc*, he drew upon all his expertise regarding Moroccan social and political organisation to outline a new direction for French policy towards the increasingly turbulent populations of North Africa; a controversial book and a flawed one, it nevertheless reveals quite strikingly the depth and the extent of Montagne's knowledge and understanding of Moroccan society.

In the same year, 1952, he began to show signs of ill-health, but he refused to reduce the extent of his activities and continued to teach and write for almost two more years. He died at home on the 26th of November 1954.[2]

* * * *

The Berbers: Their Social and Political Organisation was originally published in 1931 by the Comité de l'Afrique Française as *La Vie Sociale et La Vie Politique des Berbères*. This book was based upon a series of seminars given by Robert Montagne in 1930 at the Institut des Etudes Islamiques in the Faculté des Lettres of the University of Paris soon after the publication of his major study of Berber society— *Les Berbères et le Makhzen dans le Sud du Maroc*—which had been accepted that year by the University of Paris as a doctoral thesis. In 1947 Montagne revised the original manuscript with a view to publishing a new edition of the 1931 volume; this revised version was, however, never published. The present translation is based on this hitherto unpublished manuscript of 1947, which was kindly made available for this purpose by the Centre des Hautes Etudes d'Administration Musulmane (C.H.E.A.M.) in Paris.

In so far as this short volume represents only a summary, albeit a detailed one, of the main themes developed in *Les Berbères et le Makhzen*, it would be misplaced to attempt here a full discussion of the significance of Montagne's early sociological work in the Maghreb. It is necessary, however, to provide some indication of the social and political, as well as of the intellectual, context within which Montagne's research on the Berbers was carried out and within which both *Les Berbères et le Makhzen* and *La Vie Sociale* were written and published. It is also necessary, I believe, to comment upon the relevance of Montagne's analysis of Berber society to certain contemporary debates upon the nature of tribal politics and upon the process of state formation in pre-capitalist societies.

* * * *

The passage of time, the process of 'decolonisation' and the publication of several critical works on the recent history of anthropology have made it possible for sociologists and social anthropologists of the 1970's to look back at the work of the early colonial social scientists, both French and British, with new appreciation and new insight.[3] Social scientists have finally been obliged to apply their own craft to the examination of their own work and that of their predecessors as well as to the consideration of their own position in society and *vis-à-vis* the societies they study. As a result of this, many have now come to accept as valid for themselves as well as for others the basic hypothesis put forward by students of 'the sociology of knowledge'—namely, that "the existential situation of a group within a larger society is a factor which conditions the knowledge acquired and used by the group".[4] Such a hypothesis has direct relevance for an understanding of the work carried out by sociologists and social anthropologists in the colonies and overseas territories of the metropolitan country from which they themselves come.

It can be shown that social scientists working overseas in the territories of the various colonial empires were indeed fully integrated, both objectively and subjectively, into an overall colonial system whose frame of reference was largely external to the societies, or sectors of society, that they studied, but which itself included those societies and, to a large extent, determined their structure and organisation. The research carried out in these territories was usually intended not only to advance sociological theory but also (and in many cases primarily) to assist and to improve where possible the operation of the colonial system in general and the administration of the indigenous peoples in particular. The sort of research carried out, therefore, and even its theoretical orientations, were largely determined by the needs of the colonial administration. This close inter-relationship between social science research and administrative policy in the colonies and overseas territories was particularly marked in those instances (extremely common in both British and French colonial territories in the later years) where individuals were able to combine the role of social scientist with the position of administrator.[5]

In Britain, social anthropologists were convinced, very early on, that their discipline had much to offer the colonial administration in the way of practical advice. In 1884 the President of the Royal Anthropological Society of Great Britain and Northern Ireland (the R.A.I.) declared that

> the subject of ethnography . . . is perhaps the most practically important of the various branches of anthropology. Its importance to those who have to rule—and there are few of us now who are not called upon to bear our share of the responsibility of government—can scarcely be overestimated in an empire like this, the population of which is composed

of almost every diversity under which the human body and mind can manifest itself. . . .[6]

While twenty years later another President, Haddon, suggested that

a full knowledge of the local conditions and a sympathetic treatment of native prejudices would materially lighten the burden of government by preventing many misunderstandings and, by securing greater efficiency, would make for economy.[7]

This belief that "part of the business of the science of Sociology is to provide data which can be utilised by the practical politician"[8] is, of course, one that has been held by a great many social scientists, whether of the colonial or of the post-colonial period,[9] and it was certainly held by the early proponents of what came to be known as the British 'structural-functional school' of social anthropology, which developed around the 1920's and 1930's. Thus Radcliffe-Brown, one of the founders of this 'school' of anthropology, wrote in 1923 of South Africa (where he worked and taught for some time):

the study of the beliefs and customs of the native peoples, with the aim, not merely of reconstructing their history, but of discovering their meaning, their function, that is, the place they occupy in the mental, moral and social life, can afford great help to the missionary or the public servant who is engaged in dealing with the practical problems of the adjustment of the native civilisation that have resulted from our occupation of the country.[10]

Such views were undoubtedly shared by the majority of early administrators and social scientists in Algeria and, later, in Morocco. Indeed, the words of Radcliffe-Brown, quoted above, might well have been written by Montagne with regard to the Berbers of Morocco.

Despite this unequivocal concern on the part of British social anthropologists to promote the effective administration and the smooth running of the Empire, it has been suggested that the value of anthropology was not fully recognised by colonial governments until well into the twentieth century.[11] Certainly, in 1895 the President of the R.A.I. complained that the government had not yet seen the need to maintain an official department for the systematic accumulation of anthropological knowledge, or even to make an ethnographic survey of the Empire.[12] It is true, however, that, while the number of professional or 'academic' anthropologists officially employed as such by the colonial administration may have been exceedingly small, a few astute administrators realised quite early on that they required better and more systematic information about their subject peoples. Such

men took the initiative in demanding that anthropology be taught to
colonial officers and others working in the various parts of the
Empire, and special courses in anthropology were eventually established at Oxford and Cambridge for officers on leave and for cadets
training for the colonial service.

The situation in the French-controlled territories does not appear
to have been fundamentally different, for there too the systematic
utilisation of professional anthropologists by the colonial administration could hardly be said to have begun before the 1930's and 1940's.
Nevertheless, if we may judge by the situation in North Africa, it
would appear that the potential value of sociology and anthropology
as means of facilitating the administration and control of indigenous
peoples was recognised considerably earlier by the French than by
the British.

Official recognition of the importance for peaceful and effective
administration of having accurate and comprehensive information on
the customs and social organisation of the local inhabitants is to be
found in the creation of the *bureaux arabes* in Algeria as early as
1830-1840.[13] By the 1880's and 1890's a fair number of useful studies
of local languages and dialects, as well as of social organisation and
'traditional customs', had been carried out in Algeria by administrators and by administrators-cum-anthropologists like Hanoteau,
Letourneux, Masqueray and others.[14] These studies were to provide
an orientation, both theoretical and practical, that was to have a
considerable effect on similar studies in Morocco during the first
three or four decades of the twentieth century, and also on French
colonial policy in Morocco.

French military penetration of Morocco began seriously in the first
decade of this century. Montagne refers, in this volume, to the internal
disorganisation of the Moroccan state at the end of the nineteenth
century; it is clear that this internal situation was partly the result of
the growing European interference in Moroccan affairs as part of
'the scramble for Africa' and also that such a situation constituted a
danger to the French position in Algeria. As Lyautey wrote in 1907:

> regardless of what one might want, Morocco is a danger to the flanks
> of Algeria, and unless we evacuate from the latter, it will be necessary to
> intervene with force in Morocco, for its anarchy has a direct repercussion
> on our authority and on our Algerian interests.[15]

A French Protectorate was established in 1912 (to be shared with the
Spanish, who took the smaller northern 'zone' in the Rif) and by the

outbreak of the First World War the French had occupied almost all of the regions traditionally controlled by the Moroccan Sultan and his central government (the *makhzen*). The traditionally dissident tribal areas were pacified painfully and slowly over the next fifteen years until, by 1934-1935, the whole of Morocco was brought under French control and administration. By that time the seeds of nationalism and the later independence movement of the Istiqlal had been sown and were beginning to sprout.

The process of pacification was, for the most part, a piecemeal matter of coping with small tribal units almost one by one. As Gellner has pointed out,

> This 'pacification' was as much a political as a military affair. It was the ambition of those who engaged in it to achieve as much of it by political means as possible, and the view was expressed that ethnographic reconnaissance and exploration was the best preliminary to successful pacification. The consequence was a sociological orientation from the very start, a tradition which persisted in the administration—much of which remained military—even after pacification had been achieved.[16]

This 'sociological orientation' was officially recognised in Morocco from the outset. An Ecole Supérieure de Langue et Litterature Arabes et d'Etudes Dialectales Berbères was founded in Rabat in 1912; it was reorganised in 1920 and became the Institut des Hautes Etudes Marocaines in 1921. The Institut was designed to develop and maintain scientific research on Morocco and her peoples; to specialise in and to propagate a practical knowledge of Arabic and Berber, and of the geography, history, ethnography and 'civilisation' of Morocco. It also prepared Moroccan students for the examinations necessary for higher or professional training. This was essentially a 'school of humanities' based, to some extent, on the experience gained in the development of the Ecole de Droit in Algiers, where courses in 'droit musulman' and 'coutumes indigènes' had been given as early as the 1880's. The institution for secular and natural science studies, the Institut Scientifique Cherifien, also included a course in anthropology.

In 1917 the Direction des Affaires Indigènes was created; and shortly afterwards became the Direction des Affaires Indigènes et du Service des Renseignements. This section was directly under Lyautey himself and dealt with most of the matters of a political nature involving Moroccans. It consisted of a Service des Renseignements, a Section Historique and a Section Sociologique. It was in this last that Montagne worked for a number of years. It was run by a *directeur*, and one of its most important tasks was to handle tribal affairs, especially those relating to tribal property. The Service des Renseignements was important in that its *directeur* was the senior officer in charge of native police and also the chief of the intelligence officers, supervising all administrative and other action taken by them.[17]

Several writers have argued recently[18] that anthropology became officially respectable as far as the British colonial administration was concerned only when it had developed the systematic theoretical approach to the study of society characteristic of the 'structural-functional school' which emerged during the 1920's and 1930's to achieve full recognition in the early 1940's. The 'old' nineteenth-century anthropology of ethnology, diffusionism and evolutionism was replaced, they suggest, by the 'new' anthropology pioneered by Radcliffe-Brown and Malinowski in the 1920's and 1930's precisely because this new 'structural-functional' approach was eminently suitable for utilisation by administrators. Stauder writes, for example:

> In the context of Indirect Rule, functionalist social anthropology seemed obviously superior to the older, ethnological approach, for the 'newer' social anthropology not only concentrated on identifying and describing the key social and political institutions of a subject people, but it also attempted to analyse how these institutions worked. Those concerned with problems of administration, and knowledgeable about anthropology, came to accept the validity of Radcliffe-Brown's claims on behalf of the practical superiority of the functionalist method.[19]

If such emphasis has been laid on the significance of the development of the 'structural-functional' school of thought in British anthropology as a virtual precondition for the official acceptance of anthropology as a valuable addition to the armoury of the colonial administration, how can one explain the importance of sociology and anthropology in the French colonial administration in North Africa, where it appears to have flourished and have found official recognition earlier than it did in Britain?

It would seem that several different elements make up the answer to this question. Firstly, the theoretical development of anthropology was, almost certainly, further advanced in France than in Britain at the turn of the century. Radcliffe-Brown himself considers his 'scheme of interpretation' to have been "derived from such earlier writers as Montesquieu, Comte, Spencer and Durkheim, and thus belongs to a cultural tradition of two hundred years".[20] Raymond Aron, in his discussion of the main currents in sociological thought, concentrates upon Montesquieu, Toqueville, Comte, Marx, Pareto, Weber and

Durkheim.[21] This predominantly continental European tradition contributed to the early development in France of ideas that were only later to become absorbed into British sociological thought. The major works of the immensely influential Durkheim, for instance, were available in France by the 1890's and began almost immediately to have a considerable impact both on theoretical developments and on more practical methodological concerns within the French sociological tradition. Secondly, and importantly for the development of sociology in the colonies and other occupied territories, there appears to have been considerable contact between the workers in the field overseas and sociologists in France. Durkheim, for example, cites the work of Hanoteau and Letourneux and of Masqueray in Algeria in his work on *The Division of Labour in Society*, and their work on Kabyle tribal structure contributed much to his discussion of the differences between 'mechanical' and 'organic' solidarity.[22] On the other hand, the intellectual debt to Durkheim of such fieldworkers as Doutté (and indeed of Montagne himself) in Morocco was explicitly recognised in their own publications. Finally, in Morocco at least, and probably also in Madagascar and Indo-China, French colonial administration was by no means wedded exclusively to the concept of direct rule. Indeed, Scham writes, of Lyautey, that "he did not want men imbued with the Algerian tradition of direct administration nor did he want stolid bureaucrats, but rather thinking men with imagination and initiative".[23] His own approach to the administration of the Protectorate suggests that he took the advice given him in 1894 by the Governor-General of Indo-China, de Lanessan:

> In every country there is a social framework. The great error of the Europeans who come as conquerors is to destroy these frameworks. The country so deprived falls into anarchy. One must govern with the mandarin, and not against him. The European, not being superior in numbers, cannot take his place, but only supervise. Therefore do not offend local traditions; do not change customs. There is in every society a leadership class, born to direct the affairs of the people, without which one is powerless. Use that class in our best interests.[24]

When such a strong belief in the necessity of 'indirect rule' guides the policy of the colonial government, then sociological and anthropological research becomes not merely helpful but indispensable.

* * * *

Montagne's study of the Berbers of southern Morocco was published some thirty years after the first systematic sociological research was carried out in Morocco. During those thirty years both the policies of the colonial government and administration and the interpretation of the main features of Moroccan society underwent significant changes; these changes in government policy and sociological interpretation were closely interrelated.

The image of Morocco which one finds in the French historical and sociological literature of the 1920's and 1930's is characterised by a set of stereotypes relating to the nature of the Moroccan state and of Moroccan society. The development of this image of Moroccan society had a profound influence upon the evolution of France's Berber policy in particular as a fundamental element in the general administrative policy of the Protectorate; at the same time, this image developed, in large part, as a result of shifts in government policy. The stereotypes relate to: Moroccan Islam, the nature of the Muslim state, the quality of the Sultan's authority, the relationship between *makhzen* and *siba*, the relationship between Arabs and Berbers, and the supposed backwardness and isolation of pre-colonial Morocco. In general terms the composite stereotype comprising these elements emphasised the division of Morocco into two zones, one where the central government (the *makhzen*) was supreme, taxes were collected, governors governed and the Law was respected, and the other a region of anarchy (*siba*) where the central government was impotent and the dissident tribes spent their time in feuding and warfare. An American historian has recently described this set of stereotypes, which he terms 'the Moroccan Vulgate', as follows:

> Under the rubric 'Bled el Makhzen' and 'Bled es Siba', the portrait of a regime divided between contradictory tendencies toward autocratic order and anarchy, in which neither was able to gain the upper hand, has gained widespread acceptance. Closely interwoven with this image has been a second one, a view of a profound ethnic split in Moroccan society between Arabs and Berbers. The course of Moroccan history prior to the protectorate was seen as the efforts of the Arab government to impose themselves upon the Berber dissidents."[25]

This general picture of Moroccan society is accepted by Montagne in his analysis of Berber social and political organisation, both past and present, and his study serves to confirm many of the stereotypes mentioned above. Despite his emphasis on the need for 'objective' research based on material collected without preconception and presented initially as social 'facts' to be interpreted only later, he is as guilty as any other French colonial sociologist in Morocco at this period of distortion and bias in his general analysis, particularly when he considers Berber society 'as a historian' through the available literature, rather than 'as a sociologist' working from material collected by himself in the field.[26]

Before 1904 the image of Morocco presented by the French scholars supported by the Comité de l'Afrique Française was comparatively tentative, flexible and undogmatic. The most complete analysis of Moroccan rural society was based upon the descriptions provided by Edmond Doutté who, between 1900 and 1904, made three expeditions in the south of Morocco. On the relationship between the *bled el makhzen* and the *bled es siba* Doutté wrote in 1901:

> The characterisation of bled el Makhzen as opposed to bled es Siba is not correct, for all of Morocco under different forms and to varying degrees undergoes the action of the Makhzen. . . .[27]

Instead of insisting upon the distinction between Arabs and Berbers in Morocco Doutté minimised it, thus refusing to accept the views of many Algerian 'experts'. He argued that

> as much in Morocco as in Algeria the ethnic division of natives into 'Arabs' and 'Berbers' is a vain distinction, because no criteria can be invoked on which to base this distinction. . . . The word 'Berber' has no precise sense except a linguistic one in which it designates a group of dialects closely allied to one another.[28]

Finally, while the majority of French scholars came to regard the persistent conflict between *bled el makhzen* and *bled es siba* as clear evidence of hopeless conflict and anarchy within Moroccan society, Doutté believed that

> all this is not disorder, but a kind of order; in this apparent chaos all the living forces end up by finding an equilibrium: the play of sectional interests and coalitions of all kinds results in a kind of social equilibrium which constitutes a durable state, as much in the tribes as in the cities.[29]

Such a conception of the Moroccan state compares very interestingly with that held by certain Moroccan scholars of post-colonial Morocco.[30]

In 1904, however, France managed, in the process of 'horse-trading' among the European powers, to achieve a position of undisputed hegemony over Moroccan affairs—a position that received international recognition in 1906—and suddenly discovered that it had a certain vested interest in the Makhzen. The French believed that, by becoming identified with the Makhzen and with certain major regional 'lords', they could continue their policy of gradual penetration without arousing the antagonism either of the indigenous population or of the rival political powers. Under the stated policy of 'peaceful penetration' they sought to consolidate their position of dominance in Morocco through the introduction of a wide range of internal reforms in cooperation with the Sultan and the Makhzen.

During this period of increasing French control in Morocco the writings of the French sociologists and anthropologists underwent a distinct change. The image of the Moroccan state as a complex pattern of interaction between interest-groups and different sections of the population within the society at large and the subtly nuanced analysis of such scholars as Doutté, Aubin and others were replaced by a relatively simplistic, mechanical model of relations between *makhzen* and *siba*, between Arabs and Berbers, and between law and order and anarchy, in which the distinction between the political and religious authority of the Sultan served to emphasise the importance of these dichotomies.

Relatively little was known, however, about the Berber-speaking peoples of Morocco in the earliest stages of the French penetration and, initially at least, the stereotype of Berber society remained undeveloped. In the years following the establishment of the Protectorate, and as the French came increasingly into contact (and conflict) with the tough Berber tribesmen of the mountain regions, there evolved the romantic image of the 'noble Berber' (as opposed to the 'ignoble Arab') in much the same way as the tribesmen of the 'northwest frontier' region became, for the British in India, the stereotype of the hardy, courageous and essentially simple tribesman. During the years between 1912 and around 1920 both the 'Berber policy' and the 'Berber myth' were gradually developed. It has been suggested that the single most influential factor in the development of French policy towards the Berbers in Morocco, as in the shaping of the image of the Moroccan Berbers, was the introduction into Moroccan administrative ideology of 'the Kabyle myth'.[31]

The analysis of Kabyle society suggested that two institutions were of paramount importance in the social organisation of the Berber tribes: the *jama'a*, or council of elders, and the corpus of theory and precedent embodied in the *'urf*, or customary law. Both the *jama'a* and *'urf*, being considered crucial elements of Berber society, promised a means of controlling the Berbers without necessarily resorting to the use of force. Furthermore, the existence of these and other significant institutions were believed to mark the Berbers as clearly distinct, in terms of social structure and social organisation (as well as of language and customs), from the Arabs. Perhaps of greatest significance was the belief in the 'basically democratic spirit' of Berber society and the idea that the Berber political system was saved from complete anarchy only by the strength of their opposition to outside forces and the coherence provided by the *jama'a* and *'urf*. All these features were considered intrinsic to Berber society, whether

in Algeria or Morocco, and were felt to be eminently worth preservation both for their own sakes and for their usefulness in facilitating
the administration of the rural areas.

A special 'Berber study centre' was set up in Meknes as early as
1913, and in 1915 a Comité d'Etudes Berbères was established. The
general objective of these groups is clearly expressed in the first issue
of the *Archives Berbères* (the organ of the Comité):

> We must thoroughly study them [the Berbers]. The work done in Algeria
> and especially that of Hanoteau and Letourneux will furnish us with a
> solid base for that; but customs vary from tribe to tribe, from village to
> village; the peculiarities must be carefully noted and examined to form a
> documentary basis from which we shall be able to establish the principles
> upon which the political and administrative control of these populations
> may be founded.[32]

Underlying much of this concern to understand the basis of Berber
society was, beyond the desire to facilitate the immediate problem of
pacification and the subsequent problem of administration, a hope
that it might be possible eventually to assimilate the Berbers to
French 'civilisation' rather than merely to allow them to become
'Arabised'. After 1919-1920 the final goal of assimilation was
gradually abandoned but the policy of regarding, and treating, the
Berbers as distinct (both socially and culturally) from the Arabs and
their social institutions as worthy of preservation was maintained
until the 1930's at least. In 1930 French 'Berber policy' culminated
in the promulgation of the notorious *dahir Berbère* to which both the
editors of *La Vie Sociale et la Vie Politique* . . . and Montagne
himself allude in a number of places. This was seen by the Moroccans
as the final stage in an evolving French policy of divide and rule in
Morocco aimed at generating and clarifying a major cleavage through
Moroccan society in order to facilitate the overall control and mani-
pulation of the indigenous population. The decree was intended to
regulate the legal status of the pacified Berber tribal territories and
essentially offered those areas the option of remaining separate from
the national Muslim legal system and of retaining tribal customary
law under the supervision of the French administration.[33] The
publication of this decree and the resulting reaction from the Muslim
population may be said to mark a crucial turning point both in the
evolution of French policy and also in the development of Moroccan
self-awareness and the growth of nationalism.

*   *   *   *

Despite its clear prejudices and one-sided interpretations of
Moroccan society Montagne's study of the Berbers in the south of

Morocco remains one of the most stimulating and original pieces of research into tribal, social and political structure carried out in North Africa during the colonial period. One indication of the importance of Montagne's work on the Berbers is the extent to which his analysis of tribal politics and the process of state formation is relevant to a number of important themes in contemporary political anthropology.

It is noticeable that the great majority of British social anthropologists working in Africa during the 1930's and 1940's were concerned primarily with 'government', 'politics' and 'social control' in tribal societies. Stauder has suggested that

> such an emphasis must be seen in the light of the strategy adopted by British colonialism to implement and maintain social control over the millions of people under its government in Africa. . . . Given a necessity to economise manpower and finances in Africa, British colonial governments preferred to retain and utilise traditional political institutions. . . . But if African political institutions were to be adapted and used by colonial governments, it was imperative to understand what they were and how they worked."[34]

Similar pressures operated upon sociologists working in Morocco from 1905 onwards, and it is not surprising if Montagne's analysis of Berber society set out in this volume is concerned primarily with government, politics and social control.

The contribution made by *La Vie Sociale et La Vie Politique* . . . to our understanding of the economy of the various Berber groups, for example, is minimal, and although the relations of production and of exchange are clearly intimately related to power relations in Berber society there is little systematic consideration of these aspects of social organisation. The relations of production and the organisation of work are hardly discussed, and when such institutions as the *tuiza* and the organisation of working groups to utilise saline deposits are mentioned they are not analysed in any detail. The social significance of the collective storehouse in general and its economic function in particular are discussed at the most superficial level; it is used, rather, as an indicator of the stage reached in a general evolutionary sequence from nomadic to settled life—a suggestion that is itself highly questionable and conjectural. Markets are mentioned largely to draw attention to the difficulty of maintaining law and order outside the canton although the more general question of the exact relationship between control over economic transactions and political power is an important one.

Finally, although Montagne does recognise the far-reaching effect upon the local economy of integration into the colonial economy, and mentions specifically the way in which patterns both of production and of consumption were altered and dislocated, he fails to discuss here the extent to which Moroccan society as a whole had already been altered and affected by European intervention in 'national' politics and the 'national' economy before the military penetration and pacification.[35] His perception of the rural exodus and the growth of labour migration, both within Morocco and abroad, is, moreover, coloured by his somewhat romantic enthusiasm for the inherent 'vitality' and 'adaptability' of the Moroccan Berbers, so that he is led to regard labour migration simply as a positive and encouraging adaptation to new circumstances, rather than as a desperate and generally inadequate response to the rural economic crisis that he himself deplores.

Montagne's unwillingness to analyse in detail the relationship between economic and political factors, whether in studying the past or the present condition of Berber society, in the end condemns his valiant attempts to explain the process of state formation and the transformation of political structures to failure. In this failure he is, of course, by no means alone, for the majority of his anthropological contemporaries, and even of those who came after him, have also failed to account satisfactorily for major transformations in the political structure of 'pre-industrial' or of 'tribal' societies.[36] His attempts, moreover, and the material upon which he bases these attempts, to explain the transformation of one mode of political organisation into another are extremely interesting and valuable, not only to the student of the Maghreb, but to all students of politics in 'tribal' society.

His concern to present the analysis of Berber political organisation in both its 'static' and in its 'dynamic' aspect gives his work a strength lacking in large part from similar investigations carried out by his British contemporaries. (The relative inadequacy of the early British 'structural-functional' school in this respect may be seen even in the enormously influential collection of essays on African political systems edited by Fortes and Evans-Pritchard and published in 1940. In the introduction to this collection a distinction is made between 'state' and 'stateless' societies, but the distinction is purely typological and there is little attempt to explore the question of the evolution of political structures and their transformation from one 'type' to another. Marvin Harris has even gone so far as to suggest that the "distortions introduced by means of the synchronic focus in

African Political Systems threatened to reduce our understanding of state formation to a shambles").[37]

His willingness, at the same time, to consider tribal political organisation in the rural areas as part of a wider overall system which included both the Makhzen and the tribes, despite his primary concern with the political systems of canton and tribe (as well as his recognition and incorporation within the analysis of the effects of European penetration) gives his analysis an inclusiveness and scope often lacking from those of British anthropologists writing at the same period.

Thus Montagne manages to avoid the unnecessarily restrictive framework of the British structural-functionalists of the 1930's and 1940's by setting tribal politics in their wider social and historical context, and by considering the dynamic as well as the static (synchronic) aspects of social structure and social organisation. Like the structural-functionalists he is concerned to understand the structure of tribal society by means of the analysis of relationships between the various institutions co-existing within the society, and between the groups and individuals whose actions constitute the basis of these institutions. Unlike them, he also draws upon evolutionary approaches to the study of society and frequently attempts to develop a sort of comparative evolutionary model for the transformation of Berber social and political structures. This latter approach is fraught with difficulties and may be considered misleading and unreliable in the absence of good historical data, but it can provide fascinating insights into the dynamics of structural change.

In the 1940's and 1950's several British anthropologists expressed their dissatisfaction with the predominantly synchronic approach and one of the most influential critiques of the earlier structural-functional analyses is of particular interest in the present context. In his *Political Systems of Highland Burma* Edmund Leach attempts to analyse a region-wide process of change among the hill-tribes of Burma involving shifts from the ideally 'democratic' political organisation of the dispersed hill-tribes (Kachin), through intermediate forms, to something like the ideally stratified kingdoms of the lowlands (Shan), and vice versa; in other words he tries to establish a dynamic, 'pendulum-swing' model of social change. Running throughout Montagne's analysis of Berber political structure and organisation may be found an amazingly similar model, or thesis. He suggests for instance as a general hypothesis that

Berber society oscillates between two rival and opposed social forms, between on the one hand democratic or oligarchic tribal republics ruled by assemblies or hierarchies of assemblies, and on the other hand ephemeral tribal tyrannies, exemplified in modern times by the 'great caids' of the South.[38]

Certainly the degree of sophistication in analysis and also the detail of the data upon which the analysis is based is far greater in Leach's work than in that of Montagne, but the basic formulation is similar in both instances.

Unlike Leach, however, whose treatment of evolving political forms in highland Burma purports at least to lean upon an ecological analysis (by which Leach means studying 'variation in the resources and means of production'), Montagne pays relatively little attention to such factors as ecology or to the relationship between economic and political structures at the level of the canton or tribe. Indeed, in one passage (p. 63), he explicitly warns against assuming any direct causal relationship between, for example, the emergence of a 'centralised state' and its proximity to trade routes or its control of strategic mountain passes; this compares interestingly with Leach's comments on the crucial significance of the maintenance of control over trade routes for the concentration of political power.[39] Leach himself can be (and has been) criticised for failing to consider in sufficient detail the precise relationship between economic and socio-political factors *on the ground*. His analysis suggests an oscillation between two extreme forms of political structure and 'explains' the oscillation in terms of the contradiction at the level of ideas between the two opposed forms; he does not explain why, or under what precise conditions, changes actually take place on the ground, nor does he explain fully what forces are operating in any given situation. Such, however, was not his primary intention and he points out that his "attempt to find systemic ordering in historical events depends upon the changing evaluation of verbal categories and is, in the final analysis, illusory".[40] There is, nevertheless, in his book sufficient information relating to the ecology of the region and to certain crucial aspects of economic structure to enable one to gain some insight into the relationship between social, economic and political factors.

Montagne is concerned to explore the actual political transformations undergone by Berber society in the past and to consider, in particular, the process of state formation at various levels, with a view to making generalisations regarding this process in Berber society; but he gives the reader relatively little apart from 'political' data, and in his analysis changes in political structure are explained primarily in terms of political process—especially by the gradual rise to power of important leaders. The political behaviour of individuals, on the other hand, tends to be seen as largely determined by the nature of their 'political environment'.

Despite this tendency to circularity in his analysis there are fascinating indications throughout the book, and in Chapter IV in particular, of the factors that Montagne felt to be crucial in determining the success or failure of the would-be *amghar* or tribal leader and, therefore, of crucial significance in the process of state formation. These factors are generally seen, in his analysis, from the point of view of the ambitious individual and are, broadly, to do with (1) control over material resources and (2) control over human resources.[41] They include control of land and over the process of production, control of commerce and trade (especially trade in arms), control over the funds of the council and over the levying of taxes, accumulation of personal wealth (in the form of grain in the storehouse), acquisition of a reputation for wealth and generosity, control of close agnates, the construction of effective economic and political alliances through marriage, attraction of support from more distant kinsmen and others (notably mercenaries and hirelings), the establishment of a loyal corps of slaves and 'strangers' (mercenaries) as the basis of a standing army, imprisonment or annihilation of opponents and rivals, and the establishment of a central and regional administration (or *makhzen*). These indications are not substantially enlarged upon or analysed in depth; they remain highly suggestive hints for any further consideration of the process of state formation in 'tribal' societies in general, and in North Africa in particular.

In Montagne's view, however, "the primary factors affecting a leader's growth of power are social, and it is the Berber political game which determines the phases in the emergence of the amghar" (p. 63). Such an approach is quite similar to that adopted in the work of several contemporary political anthropologists, particularly of those recently characterised as 'the action-theorists'.[42] Two major aspects of Montagne's analysis of Berber politics foreshadow, in an extremely interesting way, models for the investigation of political structure and process developed over the last fifteen years by two social anthropologists, F. G. Bailey and F. Barth. These two aspects are (1) the analysis of the emergence of political leaders, and (2) the operation of the *leff* system of political coalitions and alliances.

Bailey has pointed out that:

equilibrium analysis, in its simpler form, does not allow for the possibility that a structure may be radically changed or quite destroyed. . . . Therefore, although equilibrium analysis and the idea of maintenance are useful analytical tools up to a point, additional tools are needed to understand social change.[43]

One such tool that he mentions is the distinction between normative and pragmatic rules (between rules that say what *ought to* occur and what actually *does* occur), which provides a variable in propositions about change; another is the idea that an 'environment' may contain rival political structures. He explains this idea further:

> An opposition party, hoping to take control after the next election, is not a rival political structure: one would-be dictator, waiting his chance to murder the incumbent dictator, is not a revolutionary but a contestant operating with the rules of that particular structure (within the same arena). But an army leader who replaces a parliamentary democracy with his own brand of guided democracy does change the rules of the game, and while he was waiting and planning his coup and organising support for it, he did constitute a rival political structure within the environment of the parliamentary democracy. . . . When the same society contains two or more rival political structures, this constitutes a *political field*.[44]

The concept of a political field containing rival political structures, and the distinction between normative and pragmatic rules, illuminate both Leach's analysis of the political systems of highland Burma and Montagne's analysis of political change among the Berber tribes of Morocco. In Berber society, as described by Montagne, the political field contains two opposed political structures: that of the 'egalitarian' republic with elected councils, and that of the autocratic regime with an overall amghar and the beginnings of a state apparatus. The complete success of one form entails the complete (although possibly temporary) disappearance of the other. In Montagne's work the two polar types are not clearly isolated and analysed separately; instead we are given a general discussion of the political field and of the opposed tendencies, or rival political structures, that struggle within it.

Bailey has suggested that every political structure has rules about personnel, which say what qualifications a man needs to occupy a political role, and he argues that most structures identify the following personnel:[45]

(a) *The political community*. This is the widest group within which competition for valued ends is controlled. Beyond this point the rules do not apply and politics is not so much a competition as a fight.

(b) *The political elite*. These are the individuals within the community entitled to compete for honours and power. The boundary between ordinary members and the elite is not always sharp, and the elite itself may contain several 'grades'.
(c) *The political teams*. The political structure also has rules specifying broadly how those who are active in politics should organise themselves into 'teams'.

In his analysis of Berber politics Montagne examines and discusses the structure and organisation of the political community, as it is defined at a number of 'levels', and describes the 'nesting' or 'encapsulated' nature of the various political communities so defined: the village, the canton, the tribe and the confederation. He also discusses the political elite, although in no great detail, and gives an impression of the competition that takes place between members of the elite. He describes the way in which the council members compete with each other for wealth and power, and provides a general model for the way in which individuals may become council members and eventually amghars. Finally, he discusses the way in which aspiring leaders try to build up a following or 'team' in their struggle for supreme power within the chosen arena, and examines the *leff* alliances and coalitions, although he makes no really systematic attempt to relate the construction of individual followings to the overall pattern of *leff* alliances in a region.

His discussion of the rise to power of ambitious individuals resembles, in a number of ways, the recent discussion of leaders and their 'teams' in Bailey's *Stratagems and Spoils* and much can be gained from comparing the two. Perhaps even more strikingly, however, there are many places in Chapters II, III and IV where the discussion recalls Barth's analysis of political leadership and political organisation among the Pathan tribesmen of Swat, in Pakistan.[46] Despite clear differences between the two situations, and the fact that the Pathans are situated at almost the other end of the Middle East from the Berbers of the Maghreb, certain aspects of Pathan tribal politics appear to resemble certain features of Berber political organisation, as described by Montagne.

Like the Berbers, the Pathans contrast the administered areas under the control of an organised central government (*hukomat*) with the areas of freedom and rebellion (*Yaghestan*), considering themselves to be part of the latter. The analysis made by Barth of politics among the Pathan is of particular interest in the present context in that it explores the relationship between the actions of would-be leaders, the followings they build up in support of their position, and the overall pattern of political alliances, or blocs, as Barth calls them, in Pathan society. Having discussed the 'basic framework' of Pathan society and the overall structure generated by the organisation of social groupings for many purposes along lines defined by agnatic descent, Barth then suggests that "intertwined with this basic frame is a system of political alliances, through which individuals by their own choice align themselves in a political dual division. The groups which for most political purposes act together as corporate units are the regional branches of these two factions or blocs."[47] Among the Pathans, as among the Berbers, members of agnatic descent groups at every recognised level of segmentation meet in councils for the purpose of governing and administering the tribal segment of which they form the core; in this way a hierarchy of councils is defined corresponding in terms of council membership to the overall structure comprising a number of 'nesting' tribal segments. But, Barth notes,

> when members align against each other in debates, or any other form of opposition they do *not* act in terms of such a merging series. In a meeting of a council of a wide area, there is *not* the fusion of interests of smaller, related segments of a minor council *vis-à-vis* larger segments which one would expect in a lineage system. . . . On the contrary, the opposition between small, closely related segments persists in the wider context, and these segments unite with similar small segments in a pattern of two-party opposition, not in a merging series of descent segments.[48]

Nearly all questions of administration among the Pathans relate to land, and the system of land tenure defines prominent lines of cleavage between agnatic collaterals. Persisting opposition between close collaterals—which generally stops short of alienating brothers —prevents their interests from fusing, even *vis-à-vis* outsiders. In fact, the political actions of a Pakhtun (a member of the land-owning class and of the political elite) are directed primarily at gaining an advantage over his agnatic rivals, as only through their defeat can he achieve his own aggrandisement. Any loss by his collaterals means a gain for him. In order to defend or advance their interests in land, members of a small cohesive group (A) will tend to seek alliance with other small but more distant groups (C, D, E) against their close collaterals (B); while their rival and hostile close collaterals (B) tend to ally themselves with the rivals of the first group's (A) allies (F, G, H). Such alliances, if widely and consistently extended, will produce a pervasive division of the region into two opposed blocs.

The Pathan blocs, or alliances (*dela*) have this structure, according to Barth's analysis and so, it would seem, have the *leffs* of the Moroccan Berbers and the *soffs* of the Algerian Kabyles (or at least something like it). The pattern of opposition and alliance that appears, in Montagne's analysis, to divide Berber society into two pervasive blocs (what Montagne terms moieties) and the famous chequer-board image itself might perhaps be explained along similar lines (with suitable modifications) to Barth's explanation of the *dela* in Pathan tribal politics.

It is important to mention at this point that Barth's 'individual-istic' approach to the analysis of Pathan political organisation, in which he is concerned primarily "to explore the kinds of relationship that are established between persons in Swat, the way in which these may be systematically manipulated to build up positions of authority, and the variety of politically corporate groups which result"[49] (and which is very similar to the approach adopted by Montagne) has been subjected to substantial reconsideration very recently by Talal Asad. This reconsideration is of direct relevance to the material discussed by Montagne, for it asks the question: if Swat political organisation is to be viewed (as Barth presents it) as a consensual rule-structured activity, who defines and applies the rules of the game? The answer given is that 'it is the Pakhtun landowners who do so',[50] and this leads the argument on to a discussion of Pathan political structure as 'individual consent and dyadic links between individuals' versus 'collective exploitation and class structure'. Here Asad argues, against Barth, that horizontal cleavages into asym-metric classes are more important than vertical ones into homologous blocs. The tenant's class interests are always opposed to those of his landlord.[51]

While, on the surface, Barth's model of Swat politics represents an anarchic, conflict-ridden, violent society, his analysis is permeated with notions of consent in at least three different senses:

1. in the sense of individual decisions, by each would-be follower or ally or chief, concerning transactions with political implica-tions;
2. in the sense of the peasant's recognition that the activity of a sovereign authority (the landowners) is necessary for the maintenance of life and security—and their acceptance of the political obligation that this recognition implies;
3. in the sense of all agreeing to the rules of the game.

Where there is domination, as between chiefs and followers, there is order and consent; where there is no domination, as between independent blocs, there is conflict and violence, according to Barth. This, suggests Asad is reminiscent of the Hobbesian model, for there is a tendency in both to see the problem of political domination and the problem of social order as being ultimately identical. In Barth's analysis, he suggests, we get the following assumption: "Swatis are competitive, acquisitive and violent, hence they must have a sovereign (i.e. authoritative rules of the game and a class that defines and sanctions those rules) if they can be said to be living an ordered social life".[52]

> For most anthropologists the basic orientation in discussion of exotic politics has been the maintenance of social order. In classic functionalist studies the focus was on total politics, and order was represented as a mechanical consequence of the relevant institutions—chiefship, law, custom, kinship, etc. In modern interactionist studies the focus is typically on segmentary politics, and order tends to be represented as a statistical consequence of a multitude of individual actions and relationships. . . . Barth's *Political Leadership among Swat Pathans* straddles these two traditions.[53]

A class analysis, it is suggested, can go further for it makes possible an approach to the problems of political domination not in terms of a consensual rule-structured order, but in terms of the dialectical relationship between different, and possibly contradictory, modes of consciousness, within developing material circumstances which are only partly controlled by such consciousness.[54]

Such suggestions open up many avenues for the student of 'tribal' politics whether in Morocco or elsewhere, but without a detailed discussion of the economic structure, the system of land tenure and the analysis of relations of domination and exploitation in rural areas as well as a far more subtle and nuanced exploration of the relations between local structures and national or super-national structures than is provided, for instance, by Montagne, an analysis along the lines suggested by Asad would be impossible.

Montagne's analysis is clearly inadequate, for a number of reasons, in terms of the demands that might be made of it in the 1970's. Despite this, however, it continues to provoke and excite by its considerable insight into certain important aspects of tribal politics and the nature (and formation) of the state in the Maghreb during the pre-colonial and early colonial periods, and also by the fact that the discussion bears directly upon problems that are still exercising sociologists and anthropologists more than forty years after the publication of his two works on the Berbers.

DAVID SEDDON

NOTES

1   Woolman, *Rebels in the Rif: Abd el Krim and the Rif Rebellion.*
2   A fuller appreciation of the life and work of Robert Montagne by a number of his friends and colleagues may be found in *L'Afrique et l'Asie* (No. 32, 1955), a Journal that he had founded and helped to edit, and to which he contributed numerous articles between 1948 and 1953.
3   Foster, *Applied Anthropology*; Harris, *The Rise of Anthropological Theory*; Mair, 'The Social Sciences in Africa South of the Sahara: the British Contribution' in *Human Organization*; Stauder, 'The Function of Functionalism: the adaptation of British social anthropology to British colonialism in Africa' (paper presented at the Meetings of the American Anthropological Association, November 1971). These are just a few of the works that have appeared.
4   Maquet, 'Objectivity in Anthropology', in *Current Anthropology*, pp. 47-48.
5   Forde, 'Applied Anthropology in Government: British Africa', in *Anthropology Today* edited by Kroeber; Mair, op. cit.
6   Quoted by Foster, op. cit., pp. 184-185.
7   Haddon, 'Presidential Address: Anthropology, its Position and Needs', in *Journal of the Royal Anthropological Institute*, Vol. 33, p. 20.
8   Haddon, ibid., p. 19.
9   The growth of 'development studies' is largely an expression of a continued wish to assist government and administration on the part of social scientists. See Apthorpe, *People, Planning and Development Studies*, p. vii; Cochrane, *Development Anthropology*.
10 Radcliffe-Brown, 'The Methods of Ethnology and Social Anthropology', in *South African Journal of Science*, Vol. 20, pp. 142-143.
11 Stauder, op. cit. passim.
12 Macalister, 'Presidential Address', in *Journal of the Royal Anthropological Institute* Vol. 24, pp. 452-468.
13 Yacono, *Les Bureaux Arabes*. Also see note 22.
14 E.g. Hanoteau and Letourneux, *La Kabylie et les Coutumes kabyles*; Masqueray, *Formation des Cités chez les Populations Sédentaires de l'Algerie.*
15 Quoted in Scham, *Lyautey in Morocco*, p. 12.
16 Gellner, *Saints of the Atlas*, p. 18.
17 Scham, op. cit., pp. 60-75, 146-161.
18 E.g. Stauder, op. cit., pp. 6, 7, 17; also see Maquet op. cit.
19 Stauder ibid., p. 17; also see Harris, op. cit., pp. 514-567.
20 Radcliffe-Brown, Introduction to *Structure and Function in Primitive Societies*, p. 14.
21 Aron, *Main Currents in Sociological Thought*.
22 Durkheim, *The Division of Labor in Society*, pp. 174-199. My argument regarding the significance of "considerable contact between workers in the field overseas and sociologists in France" may go beyond the evidence presently available. The argument involves a distinction between 'professional anthropologists' and 'ideas developed in sociology and anthropology'; I suggest that the French colonial administration made use of the 'ideas of sociology and anthropology' earlier than did the British, although there can be little doubt that, from the 1930's onwards, that the connection between the universities (and university anthropologists) and the colonial administration was probably greater and certainly more systematically developed in Britain than in France. The subject, however is complex and requires further investigation before a valid comparison can be made. I hope to explore the subject further in a future publication.

23 Scham, op. cit., pp. 48-49.
24 Maurois, *Lyautey*, p. 54.
25 Burke, 'The Image of the Moroccan State in French Historical Literature: New Light on the Origins of Lyautey's Berber Policy', in *Arabs and Berbers*, edited by Gellner and Micaud (page references are to the unpublished MS.) p. 2.
26 For some discussion of distortion in the presentation of Moroccan history, see Lacoste, *Ibn Khaldun: naissance de l'histoire passé du tiers monde*; also Sahli, *Décoloniser l'Histoire: introduction à l'histoire du Maghreb*. (Chapter 4).
27 Doutté, 'Une Mission d'Etudes', in *Renseignements Coloniaux*, 1901, p. 171.
28 Doutté, ibid., p. 166.
29 Doutté, ibid., p. 172.
30 E.g. Lahbabi, *Le Gouvernement Marocain à l'Aube du XXe Siècle*; Waterbury, *The Commander of the Faithful*, Chapters 1 and 3.
31 Cf. Burke, op. cit., p. 28.
32 Simon, 'Les études berbères au Maroc et leurs applications en matière de politique et de l'administration', in *Archives Berbères*, I, 1915, pp. 4-5.
33 Cf. Gellner, op. cit., pp. 18-19.
34 Stauder, op. cit., pp. 16-17.
35 Cf. Montagne, *Les Berbères et le Makhzen dans le Sud du Maroc*, pp. 46-48. Here he mentions the devastating effect on the economy of southern Morocco of the penetration of the Moroccan economy by European enterprise and of Morocco's increasing involvement in the international market.
36 It is clearly impossible here to place Montagne's analysis within the general discussion, reaching back now over a hundred years, of the process of state formation. Lewis Morgan, Engels, Lowie and Malinowski all make valuable contributions and Krader's *Formation of the State* runs quickly over some of the better-known views on the subject. I hope to consider the transformation of political structures among the Berbers in greater detail in a future publication.
37 Harris, op. cit., p. 537.
38 Gellner, op. cit., p. 26.
39 Leach, *Political Systems of Highland Burma*, p. 237. "The trade routes through the mountain barrier . . . have been of importance for centuries and the bulk of the population has long resided on or close to these east-west tracks through the mountains. Income from tolls from transit caravans was in the past an important element in the economy of the whole zone. It was the major source of power of the leading *gumsa* chiefs in the 19th century, just as in zone A rice land and slaves were a major source of power." Referring to the three Lords of the Atlas, Jamil Abun Nasr points out that "the wealthiest of the three was the Glawa chieftaincy, whose control of a salt mine at Talwat (Telouat) attracted trans-Saharan traders to it" (*A History of the Maghrib*, p. 299).
40 Leach, op. cit., p. xii.
41 Cf. Meillassoux, 'From reproduction to production: a Marxist approach to economic anthropology', in *Economy and Society*, Vol. 1, No. 1, pp. 93-105.
42 Cf. Cohen, 'Political anthropology: the analysis of the symbolism of power relations', in *Man* (*NS*), Vol. 4, No. 2, p. 223.
43 Bailey, *Stratagems and Spoils*, pp. 14-15.
44 Ibid., p. 16.
45 Ibid., p. 23.
46 Barth, *Political Leadership among Swat Pathans*; also Barth, 'Segmentary opposition and the theory of games: a study of Pathan organization', in *Journal of the Royal Anthropological Institute*, Vol. 89, pt. 1.

47 Barth, 'Segmentary opposition . . .', pp. 6-7.
48 Ibid., p. 9.
49 Barth, *Political Leadership*, p. 2.
50 Asad, 'Market model, class structure and consent: a reconsideration of Swat political organisation', *Man (NS)*, Vol. 7, No. 1, p. 82.
51 Ibid., p. 85.
52 Ibid., p. 92. Such a discussion at the level of the 'tribe' may be linked to the similar discussion at the level of 'the Moroccan state' alluded to in Gellner, *Saints of the Atlas*. (The two are intimately related). See pp. 22-29.
53 Ibid., p. 93.
54 Ibid., p. 93.

Introduction to the 1931 Edition by its Editors

Twenty years ago, shortly after the removal of Mulay 'Abd el 'Aziz from power, *L'Afrique Française*[1] published a penetrating study by the late E. Doutté, under the title: *The Causes of a Sultan's Downfall*. In this book, Doutté, a pioneer of ethnography in Morocco —who has, since 1905, given us a fine monograph on *The Social and Domestic Organisation of the Haha*, and two other interesting works: *Marrakesh* and *Among the Tribes*—revealed some of the most characteristic features of social life in the Sherifian Empire, which was still poorly known at that time.

A great deal has happened since then. The success of our efforts to pacify the country has enabled us to leave the plains, to advance into the mountain regions, and to make prolonged contact with the primitive people of the high valleys in areas which the early travellers had been able only to pass through at speed. At the same time as the country was being opened up, scientific studies were becoming better organised. The Institut des Hautes Etudes Marocaines, under the energetic direction of Henri Basset, continued with remarkable vigour the investigations begun in Algeria by Hanoteau, Masqueray and René Basset. As a result of these developments there was produced, in the years between 1920 and 1930, a series of partial syntheses, each one of which threw new light upon the ancient Mediterranean world that had remained so much the same since the centuries before the Roman conquest.

One of this 'second wave' of research workers, Robert Montagne— a scholar and man of action (who was director of studies at the Institut des Hautes Etudes Marocaines as well as being attached to the Direction des Affaires Indigènes)—a few months ago completed his important work on *The Berbers and the Makhzen*,[2] which set out the results of six years' historical and sociological research undertaken in the least-known areas of the Suss and of the Rif. We reported at the time how the University of Paris praised this doctoral thesis as being the Moroccan equivalent of Masqueray's study of the formation of cities among the sedentary peoples of Algeria. It was then that the Institut d'Etudes Islamiques in the Faculté des

xli

Lettres had the happy idea of asking M. Montagne to draw together the main conclusions of his work in a series of seminars. The
notes for this series provide the basis of the short work presented
here.

The picture they give completes that sketched by Doutté more
than twenty years before. The somewhat conventional image of
the Moroccan Empire, as it appeared to observers confined to the
plains—obliged, as they were, to study Berber society from the
narrow windows that opened upon the mountains from the massive
ramparts of the Makhzen—is replaced here by the vast social and
historical panorama that one obtains from the high places of the
Atlas when one attempts to reconstruct the free and natural existence
of the ancient peoples of the Maghreb from among the independent
tribes themselves.

The seminars given by M. Montagne at the Institut d'Etudes
Islamiques were followed by those of his colleague, M. Bruno
(director of studies at the Institut des Hautes Etudes Marocaines), on
Berber customary law. The first series had prepared the audience for
the second, and we were happily surprised to see numerous Muslim
students from North Africa crowded on to the benches of the Sorbonne,
for they are normally a little uninterested in studies of simple rural
populations. It would seem that these young people were eager to
hear the conclusions reached by impartial observers, guided by a rigorous scientific methodology, on a question which, at the time, was producing the most unexpected reactions throughout the Muslim world.[3]
We were extremely pleased that they would have this opportunity to
learn about and to consider the true nature of Berber society.

For many centuries, in effect, the Middle East knew only enough of
the Maghreb to despise its inhabitants, and if quite recently it has
discovered their existence, it is in a guise that says more about the
imagination of Arab journalists than about their concern for the
truth. We have recently seen, for instance, a veritable outburst of
reaction, in the towns of the Middle East, to the announcement of a
legal reform involving no more than the administrative strengthening
of simple judicial assemblies in the Berber areas. Within the Sherifian
Empire itself cleverly organised demonstrations—which took place
even in the mosques—did their best to make the French attempts to
improve the administration of the country as unpopular as possible;
while throughout the rest of the Muslim world, from Egypt to the
Dutch East Indies, there spread the extraordinary rumour that the
High Atlas had been invaded by an army of six hundred Christian

missionaries. France, it was said, was trying to convert the Berbers to the Catholic faith.

It is certainly not difficult to take advantage of the credulity of the masses in the Middle East, but, just because such absurd fabrications have been widely believed as a result of ignorance, it is essential that both Frenchmen and Muslims should make a major effort to understand the real aspirations of the Berbers. It is this crucial task that M. Montagne tries to facilitate by his presentation, in the pages that follow, of some of the most interesting features of the social organisation of these indigenous African peoples.

Although attempts were made during the Arab Middle Ages— which in the Maghreb lasted from the eighth to the twentieth century —to obliterate all traces of the characteristic indigenous Berber culture, it retained, nevertheless, in its core, certain deep-seated aspirations which, though they may have remained hidden throughout centuries of anarchy, can be drawn out quite clearly by historical and sociological research. There is no doubt that the response of this people to contact with Western civilisation was quite particular. The 'conception' of the Protectorate involves, as far as colonial policy is concerned, not only a respect for local institutions, but also, and perhaps even more importantly, a desire to preserve unspoiled the potential which underdeveloped societies have for development, so that by raising themselves up and educating themselves they will discover for themselves the way best suited to the intellectual and moral aptitudes of their members. One may be sure that the Berbers, who have given such evidence throughout their history of their ability to resist and of their attachment to their traditional ways, will develop in the future without necessarily becoming either like the Arabs or like the French from the metropolitan country.

The troubled episode of the 'reform of Berber law' should not disturb us at all regarding the conditions under which the inevitable transformation of North African society will take place. A simple administrative reform without (and this has been poorly understood, even by the French themselves on some occasions) any political or religious significance, it marks only the first, somewhat hesitant step —taken during a period of difficulties elsewhere—in a process of almost inevitable evolution. The role of our country is to steer this process without fear or hesitation within the framework of general consensus and with full consideration for the beliefs and feelings of the people concerned.

Given this two-fold condition, the work undertaken runs little risk of being impeded, because it answers a thousand-year-old desire of a people endowed with infinite resources of patience, of application to their work and of love for their native soil, and who, besides these basic qualities, have a remarkable aptitude for collective organisation and communal life.

Let us hope that the following pages will help to remove any prejudice or hesitation which may remain, even among those of good faith. Also that they will add to our understanding of the principles upon which the future organisation of Berber society must be based, in order that it may, after centuries of war and anarchy, receive the benefits of the peace brought by the French.

NOTES

1   This was perhaps the most important of the French periodicals and journals devoted to colonial affairs.
2   This major work, of which the present volume is a summary and an abstract, was published in 1930 as *Les Berbères et le Makhzen dans le Sud du Maroc: essai sur la transformation politique des Berbères sédentaires (groupe chleuh)*.
3   This and later paragraphs refer to responses by the local Muslim population (and in other Muslim countries) to French attempts to reform the Moroccan judicial system by retaining the 'customary law' (*'urf*) in Berber areas. These attempts, which were viewed as part of a policy of 'divide and rule', culminated in the notorious Berber *dahir* (or decree) of 16th May 1930. For further comment see my Introduction.

I

Berber Society in the Maghreb and the Formation of the Sherifian Empire

Ibn Khaldun, the only Muslim historian to encompass within a single sweep the whole troubled history of Maghreb society through several centuries, formulates an hypothesis regarding the Berbers, in a famous passage in the *Kitab al-'Ibar*,[1] whose powerful insight we have not always recognised. "They belong", he tells us, "to a powerful, formidable, brave and numerous people; a true people like so many others the world has seen—like the Arabs, the Persians, the Greeks and the Romans." But the great writer immediately adds this rider, whose validity has not diminished since the fourteenth century: "Such *was* the Berber race. But, having fallen into decadence, and having lost their nationalistic spirit through the luxurious life that the exercise of power and the habit of domination had permitted to develop, their numbers decreased, their patriotic fervour diminished, and their corporate identity became weakened, to the point where the various peoples who made up the Berber race have now become the subject peoples of other rulers and bow like slaves under the burden of taxation."

In fact, the Berbers are, even today, a great people, but the tribes which comprise 'Barbary', from western Egypt to Morocco and Senegal, are scattered throughout the different regions of North Africa, "like the *membra disjecta* of a nation" in the words of Ibn Khaldun. Nevertheless, they retain a common heritage of language, of thought and of primitive art intact in the midst of the Arab populations which separate them one from another; they retain the same fundamental basis of social and political organisation, as well as their own intellectual inclinations and emotional make-up. One can say further that they have retained a profoundly original form of

D

MAP 1

The region in which the Berber language was spoken has broken up and become highly fragmented over the centuries. The principal centres remaining of some significance today are to be found in Morocco and the Sahara. It is necessary to point out, however, that the latter concentration (constituted largely by the Tuareg group) is, despite its demonstrable size, much less important than the former because of its extremely low population density. The Arabic language has spread through the entire Arabian Peninsula and the whole of North Africa. *Source: Meillet and Cohen: Les Langues du Monde.*

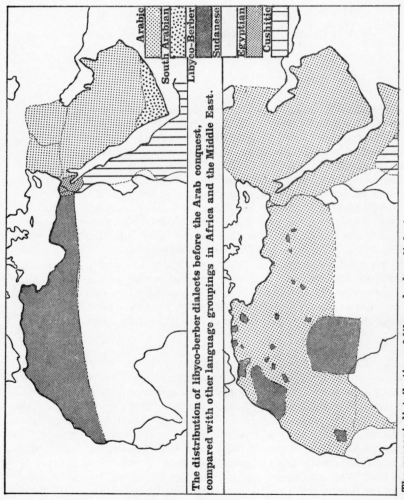

The distribution of libyco-berber dialects before the Arab conquest, compared with other language groupings in Africa and the Middle East.

The present distribution of libyco-berber dialects.

collective life, On these grounds, then, they are still a "brave and numerous" and great people.

But even if the Berbers have resisted the rising tide of Arab civilisation from their mountain fastnesses up until the present day, it is certainly true that the entire history of the Maghreb has been dominated, for more than a thousand years, by the same process: the slow destruction of indigenous institutions and the progressive assimilation of the indigenous African populations by Arab tribes and by Islamic civilisation. It is the political and social aspect of their struggle against these forces that we intend to explore in the following pages. We hope to demonstrate how Berber society has continued to show an indestructible vitality, even in our own century, and despite its decadence.

We shall be concerned initially to investigate and to describe what different linguistic, religious and political forms the attack on the Berber way of life took during the course of history, and our examples will be drawn repeatedly from that particular region of the Maghreb that we call today Morocco, for it is there that appear to be concentrated with the greatest energy and at the same time both the forces of destruction and the forces of renewal.

The Linguistic Distribution of the Berbers

Let us look now at the linguistic map of North Africa, for the retreat of Berber society can be demonstrated most clearly by means of the linguistic evidence. In this way we shall be able to judge at a glance the importance of the changes that have taken place since antiquity. Let us refer, for example, to the maps given in *Les Langues du Monde*, edited by Meillet and Cohen,[2] which are more eloquent than a long historical narrative (see Map 1).

In the fifth century BC, before the Roman conquest, the Berber peoples—the Libyans, the 'Getules', and the 'Troglodytes' of whom Herodotus and Hanno write—were in contact throughout northern Africa with 'Nigritia', the country of the 'Ethiopians'. Then, later, when they had become Romanised, or else had undergone the influence of the Carthaginians on the coast, they pushed the peaceful black populations of the oases back towards the southern regions of the Sahara. It was at about the time when the Berbers had thrust back and destroyed the 'Ethiopians' that the Arabs made their first appearance in the Maghreb. First of all, and indeed until the tenth century, they presented themselves only as political and religious

MAP 2

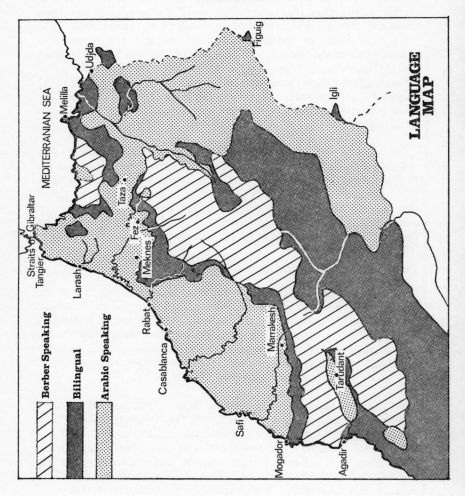

leaders, and the language they spoke was spread only by the diffusion of the Islamic faith. Then, between the tenth and the fifteenth centuries, they became invaders and pushed towards the extreme west of the Maghreb in two waves: that of the Hilal, who came for the most part via the Tell, and that of the Ma'qil, who came up from the fringes of the desert.[3] The results of these incursions by the Arabs may be seen on any twentieth-century map.

Today the Berbers have retained their language—the guardian of their traditions and of their laws—only in the mountains, in the oases of the Sahara, or in the inaccessible depths of the desert. The principal groupings are those of the Jebel Nefusa, of the Aures, of the Jurjura Kabylia, of the Rif, of the Western Atlas, of the Middle Atlas and of the Suss. The Zenaga, on the borders of Senegal, number only a few tens of thousands, while the Tuareg, despite the size of their territory, are only a few thousand. Almost everywhere the spread of the Arabic language is marked, if perhaps slow. Doutté and E. F. Gautier have estimated that in Algeria Arabic is gaining 40,000 converts every fifty years. It is clear that at other periods in the past its progress has been more rapid still.

One can see that only in one single region of the Maghreb have the indigenous African populations retained their own dialects over a sizeable territory and in large numbers, and that is the mountain regions of Morocco against which the tide of the Arab invasion was halted. A linguistic map of Morocco will enable us to clarify the relationship between the different linguistic 'forces' in operation (see Map 2). Three areas can be identified: that of Arabic speech, that of Berber, and that of bilingualism. The area where Arabic is used is, generally speaking, that of the Atlantic plains, together with the Fes-Taza corridor and the desert regions. All the towns in Morocco fall within the Arabic-speaking area. Tarudant, the capital of the Suss—which is one of the heartlands of Berber culture—is surrounded by Arabic-speaking tribes: the Ulad Yahia, Menabbha and Hauara. We should mention specifically—and we shall make this point again later—that the huge area of the Atlantic plains is not inhabited entirely by groups of Arab origin, for there are certainly many tribes which were originally Berber. In the south, for example, there are the Dukkala and the Shiadma, who were still Berber-speaking in the fourteenth and fifteenth centuries; in the north there are the tribes of the Jbala, which were probably Arabised much earlier as a result of influences from Andalusia.

The area where Berber is used exclusively is, speaking broadly, that

MAP 3

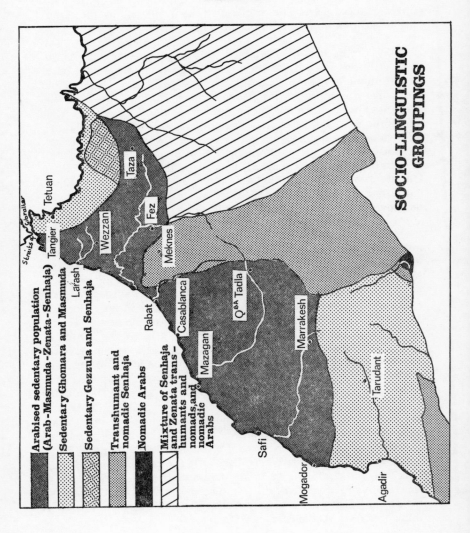

SOCIO-LINGUISTIC GROUPINGS

Arabised sedentary population
(Arab-Masmuda-Zenata-Senhaja)

Sedentary Ghomara and Masmuda

Sedentary Gezzula and Senhaja

Transhumant and
nomadic Senhaja

Nomadic Arabs

Mixture of Senhaja
and Zenata trans-
humants and
nomads, and
nomadic
Arabs

Straits of Gibraltar
Tetuan
Tangier
Wezzan
Taza
Fez
Larash
Meknes
Rabat
Casablanca
Qᵇᴬ Tadla
Mazagan
Marrakesh
Tarudant
Safi
Mogador
Agadir

of the high mountains, in the Rif and the Atlas; these are the last bastions of the linguistic resistance. The bilingual regions start at the edges of these areas. Here the women will speak Berber, while the men—or at least those whose occupations bring them in contact with the outside world—understand Arabic. One might say that this is the area where the Berber type of life, driven from the public sector and deprived of its freedom, has found refuge in the home.

One can estimate that, out of six million inhabitants—and this is a very rough figure—about two and a half million maintain their use of Berber, whether in all fields of activity or merely in the home. A crude map of population distribution in Morocco supports these suggestions (see Map 3). We can distinguish:

1. The region of the Shleuh proper, who belong for the most part to great Berber families: the Masmuda and the Gezzula between the Wed Dra and the Atlantic, to the south of Marrakesh. This is a region inhabited by sedentary populations, living in villages and hamlets which, in the high mountain areas, continue to use the fortress storehouses called '*agadirs*'. The men of this region are hard-working and frugal; it is the area which, together with the Jurjura Kabylia, provides a massive labour force for France and the rest of North Africa.

2. The region of the Senhaja: transhumants of the Jebel Saghro and Jebel Aiashi who extend as far as the Middle Atlas and the plains of the Gharb. They make use both of tents and of '*qasbahs*' (*igherm*, *tighermt*). This region is the land of sheep farmers, fierce and savage warriors upon whom Maurice Le Glay modelled his heroes.[4] It is among these people that the tradition of Berber independence is best preserved.

3. The region of the transhumant Zeneta, who live mingled with Senhaja and Arab elements all along the Muluia up to the fringes of the eastern Rif. They live in tents and have no qasbahs. These pastoralists are frequently as difficult to control as the last group (2).

4. The region of settled farmers in the north of Morocco, where Ghomara and Senhaja intermingle. They tend to live in villages or else in scattered homesteads. Like the Shleuh they practise seasonal labour migration, although in this case it is directed largely towards Algeria.

5. The Arabised region of the plains, inhabited by sedentary populations of Arab (Hilal and Ma'qil) origin—particularly near the towns—and Berbers of various different 'families'. A precise ethnic map would enable one to recognise elements from the four groups given above.

A rough classification of the tribes* made on the basis of their origins enables one to calculate the following numerical distribution: between ten and fifteen per cent of the tribes of Morocco are of genuine Arab origin. Examples are provided by the Ulad Jerrar, Menabbha and Ulad Yahia in the Suss, the Rehamna, Beni Meskin, Ahmar, Ulad bu Seba and Beni 'Amir in the Atlantic plains, and the Sofian, Khlot and Haiaïna in the Gharb. Even among these tribes we can distinguish the presence of discrete elements of Berber origin. Between forty and forty-five per cent of the tribes are Arabised Berbers, who may often claim to be Arabs but who can be assigned, on the basis of certain historical evidence, to one or other of the great Berber 'families'. These tribes often contain Arab elements, whether families or whole fractions. Examples in this category are the 'Abda, the Shawia and the Dukkala, or the *gīsh*[5] of the towns, like the Ida u Blal and the Mejjat, or the tribes of the Sahara, like the Tekna. Finally, between forty and forty-five per cent are Berber tribes within which Arab elements constitute only a tiny minority.

It can be seen that the area where Arabic is spoken is that dominated by the towns, while Berber is exclusively a rural language. The phenomenon of Arabisation is, in fact, directly related to the influence of the urban areas on the surrounding tribes, and also to the influence of the Arab tribes gathered in these areas by the Sultans. There are many towns where Berber is spoken, but there are no city-dwellers who cannot speak Arabic. Arabic, because of its universal value, is the language used for the various transactions which take place between tribes speaking different Berber dialects, as well as being the language of religion and of the central government.

Islam in Berber society

In what form is the Muslim religion introduced to the indigenous African population? It is necessary, at this point, and in order to avoid confusion and mistakes, to indicate clearly what are the major general features of Berber Islam. It has sometimes been said, with singular inaccuracy, that France drove the Berbers to Islam in North Africa and that she thereby made a serious political error by in-advertently reinforcing the barriers between these primitive peoples and our own civilisation with the unassailable bulwark of a religion which has frequently shown itself to be particularly uncompromising, and even hostile, towards the West. France had no need to encourage the Islamisation of the Berbers for the simple reason that the Berbers

* The percentages which follow can only be suggestive. No precise quantification can be attempted as long as the ethnic map of Morocco remains incomplete.

had been Islamised centuries ago.[6] Their devotion to their faith is often even more noticeable than that of the Arabs. And they would certainly be astonished if they heard, from the fastnesses of their mountain retreats, that certain ill-informed Christians or Muslims in the towns hoped, or feared, that they might be converted to the Christian faith. In Berber areas, moreover, the religion has freely assumed a quite particular form, for the tribes have adapted it over the centuries to their own intellectual and political requirements.

It is known that Islam was not accepted without a great deal of resistance on the part of the Berbers during the first three centuries of the Hejira. Their opposition first of all took on a dual form: either they established heterodox sects—as the Persians did in the Middle East—to escape the constraints of the new religion, or else, on the contrary, they adopted a rigorous puritanism and called for an even stricter doctrine in reaction against the orthodox Islam of the towns, as a way of closing their homelands off from all external intervention. Moroccan heterodoxy had a brilliant career at first, and in fact until the eleventh century, with the false prophets of Berghuata, who translated an unusual version of the Qur'an into Berber and regarding whom Ibn Khaldun has left us certain details. It appears that Jewish influences played a significant part in the foundation of this ephemeral Berber religion. No less strange were Ha-Mim—false prophet of the Ghomara—and his kinsmen, who were able, by means of magical practices, to rally the mountain-dwellers of the Rif to their support, for a period of time at least. One should probably compare this religious 'resistance' with that which developed in the Atlas mountains under the name of Judaism and which appears to have been followed secretly until after the sixteenth century. In the absence of precise documentation one might surmise that the most independent of the Berber tribes (the Zeneta of the territory of the Beni Warain, the Senhaja of the Central Atlas and the sedentary populations of the Anti-Atlas) had the intention in the early centuries of turning aside the thrust of Islam by presenting themselves as Jews—who, in the eyes of the Muslims, were privileged as 'people of the book' (*Ahl al-Kitab*) and were distinguished from pagans who might, for their lack of faith, be put to the sword or sold into slavery. What appears to support this hypothesis is the fact that, even today, one finds the best-preserved traditions of Berber magic and the richest folk-lore among Muslim tribes regarded as being of Jewish origin, despite the fact that no traces of Judaism were previously observed in their traditions. These apparently Jewish tribes would therefore have been groups of Berber origin who put up a strong resistance during the first period of Islamisation. We know, furthermore, that in the time of Leo

Africanus, at the beginning of the sixteenth century, there still remained, in several places in the Atlas, communities of Jews (or communities which were regarded as such) who owned land there and were prepared to defend it. One might suggest that these were the last remnants of Berber tribes which had, at an earlier date, taken up Judaism as a defence against the Muslim conquest.

The Berber tendency towards puritanism and austerity demonstrates a similar continuity. We should remember in this connection the tremendous success of Kharijism in the first century of Islam in the Maghreb, the existence of the little Kharijite states of Tiaret, and the establishment of the towns of the Mzab. It was in the name of a purer Islam that the Almoravids, nomadic Berbers from the Sahara, took over control of the far west of the Maghreb in the eleventh century. At the beginning of the following century, the reformer Ibn Tumert appeared in his turn to reproach his predecessors for the feebleness of their Islam and to re-establish the reign of virtue.[7] Here too, the renovation of religious beliefs and practices served as a device to obscure the reality of a Berber conquest made to the exclusive advantage of the Masmudian tribes of the western High Atlas. This ancient Kharijite and puritan strain in Berber Islam is not exhausted, even now; it reappeared in singular fashion when the people of the Maghreb became fascinated by the Wahabi sect of Nedj. 'Abd el Krim, the Berber hero of the fight for Riffian independence, seemed to favour this new simplified Islam, and the young people of Fes, although steeped in 'modern ideas', are also drawn towards the disciples of the austere Ibn Taimia. Perhaps they too are yielding, without being fully aware of it, to one of the most secret and most durable tendencies within the Berber personality.[8]

It was by founding religious kingdoms, or 'maraboutic' states, however, that the Berbers managed most successfully to reconcile Islam with their traditional social organisation.[9] Rather than attempt here to enumerate in full the religious states which appeared throughout the history of the Maghreb, let us merely cite a few. There was, for instance, that of Tit, near Mazagan, where the Beni Amghar appear to have united all the Berbers of the Tamesna region —including the great plains of the Dukkala and the Shawia, which are now Arabised—after the eleventh century on behalf of the *marabouts*. Later came the religious leaders of Safi: Sidi Mohammed Salah and his successors then the Regagra in the fourteenth century, and the disciples of the Immam Sidi Mohammed ben Sliman el Jazuli in the middle of the fifteenth, in the region of Mogador. Later still, around the middle of the sixteenth century, there appeared the marabouts of the Haha: Sidi Said ben 'Abd en-Naim and his descendants, and Sidi 'Ali, grandson of Sidi Ahmed u Musa of Tazerualt, the great saint of the Anti-Atlas, and then the Sa'dian leaders of the Dra region, the masters of the Suss. In the seventeenth century the maraboutic kingdom of Dila grew up at the foot of the Middle Atlas and spread over both flanks of the mountains and into the plains and, for a short while, threatened the towns of the north. Just at that moment the Filalian *shorfa* swept it into non-existence and seized power.[10]

A few years ago, before the establishment of the Protectorate, it was still possible to observe the state of Tazerualt in operation (although it is true that it had been declining since 1880), and also that of the marabouts of Ahansal, to the east of Demnat. In the Rif, and for the most part among the Jbala, were the kingdom of the Derkawa among the Beni Zerwal, that of Raisuli, not far from the sacred mountain of Jebel 'Alam, and that of the Khemalsha near Targist. Even recently, for instance, it was one of the leaders of the ancient 'family' of the Ahansal, Si Hausin u Temga, who led the resistance against us in the Central Atlas, while a son of the sorcerer and marabout Ma el 'Ainin, Merebbi Rebbo, acted as a comic-opera Sultan for the unpacified tribes of the Anti-Atlas.

All these maraboutic states have crucial features in common: all are based on the support of Berber communities independent of the central power. The religious leader thus appears as an arbitrator of local disputes and a benevolent protector of the mountain 'republics'. He respects their traditions and their customs, even those which are not in accord with the precepts of the Holy Book. He collects, without any difficulty, contributions which are freely offered him and rules by means of persuasion and skilful manoeuvres. His word is respected and feared because of the magic powers held by members of his lineage and because he has the power to bring the implacable curse of Allah upon the insubordinate.

The words written by Saugnier about the marabout lord of Tazerualt in the eighteenth century would certainly apply to each of these religious leaders within his own state boundaries: "This man, without any army at his disposition, is nevertheless the most powerful in all Africa. His authority is limitless. If he orders war against the Sultan of Morocco he is obeyed; and the war ceases when he wishes it. Owning nothing particular of his own, he has power over all things. Each family gives him a present every year; they vie with each other to make it worthy of note. He dispenses justice to all; he lays the accusations before his Council and, several days later, pronounces definitively. He exacts nothing from anyone, and everyone gives freely to him."

At the same time, thanks to the influence of the religious leader, Islam gradually strengthens its hold over the people. The learned become more numerous and with them the schools of Qur'anic law; little by little the traditions come to resemble those authorised by the Holy Book, and the Shari'a replaces the customary law (*'urf*) in all contexts, even those involving only the family. Henceforward, religious law intervenes in inheritance and regulates the status of women.

There is thus a true symbiosis between Islam and independent Berber society under the rule of the marabout leaders. Under this alliance the tribal political organisation remains virtually intact. In order to avoid subjection to the Sultan—that stranger who rules in the Arab towns—the people of the mountains range themselves voluntarily around a religious lord who respects the authority of the assemblies of notables, at least to all appearances. It is possible to see, moreover, how, in the course of history, the regions in which maraboutic states are established shift in direct relation to the extent of the central government's authority.

In the region of Marrakesh, for four centuries, the religious states moved ceaselessly southwards, from Safi towards the southern slopes of the Anti-Atlas, as the power of the Sultan became more extensive. These states are no longer to be found, since Spain has managed to pacify the zone over which she was given authority by treaty, except on the edges of the Sahara or in the last unpacified areas high up in the Central Atlas. This progressive retreat of Berber maraboutism reveals one of its most characteristic features, and one that has been too little stressed in the past; it emerges as one of the forms of resistance to the Makhzen, the central power. Since, however, it already brings about a complete penetration of the countryside by Islamic law—upon which the Sultan himself implicitly relies—we suggest that maraboutism already heralds the transformation of Berber society. It represents a 'pre-Makhzen' form of political organisation.

Political conquest and Berber society

Arabisation—a linguistic phenomenon—and Islamisation—a phenomenon at the same time both religious and political—are only secondary or derivative aspects of a more complete transformation of the Berber regions: that produced by the growing power of the Makhzen (the central government).[11] It is this Makhzenisation—if we may utilise such a neologism—which alone is responsible for all the other developments and which completes them and makes them final. The millennial task of the Makhzen has been to break the structure of the small independent Berber 'republics'; to bring all tribes—each with its distinctive features—within the embrace of a single, unified empire, under the same law and under the same absolute ruler. Pursued with unwearying tenacity over many centuries, this effort has resulted in the elimination of indigenous institutions throughout the vast region of the Atlantic plains where most of the towns are; the Arabised zone, a region which coincides almost exactly with the ancient Bled el Makhzen. It is the political aspect of this process of destruction above all else that we shall analyse in more detail. For the moment let us merely recall the major stages in the historical process.

What has been the unifying achievement of each of the great dynasties which have succeeded one another in the capital cities of the western Maghreb for more than ten centuries? The dynastic history of Morocco begins in the time of Moulay Idris. Moulay Idris the first, founder of the picturesque little town of Zerhun, which has retained his name, was a religious leader—today we might call him a maraboutic chief—who had received support from two Berber tribes, the Maghila and the Aureba, who were probably pastoralists from eastern 'Barbary'. He conquered the regions that are Arabic-speaking today, but at that time were probably inhabited by settled Berber populations, and which form the corridor of open country between Rabat-Sala and Tlemsen. His son, while retaining the services of the faithful Aureba, hired a guard of five hundred Arabs, descendants of the first Syrian troops who came into Africa from the north, and founded the city of Fes.

It is probable that, before him, Fes was no more than a humble township, built on the site of a little Roman town, inhabited by Jewish shopkeepers and visited periodically by the Berbers of the mountains, as is the case even today with Sefru. Moulay Idris built there a mosque and a defensive wall, and thus sowed in the heart of the city the two-fold seed of Islam and of the Arabic language which was to germinate slowly over the long centuries.

Idris was obliged to deal with the Berber areas, which were still given over to animism or else subjected to Jewish and Christian influences; he did not attempt to conquer the countryside by force, but sent his son to bear his *baraka*[12] through the various provinces, as far as the northern shores of the Rif and the most distant parts of the plains of the Suss. Soon afterwards, however, this vast maraboutic state had disappeared. It fell then to the Beni Ifren, another group of Zeneta Berbers, who came from the east through the Taza corridor, to found a secular state. The capital of this new state, and quite a modest one, was Salé. The Beni Ifren took up the struggle against the Berbers, both settled and nomadic, who at that time inhabited the Atlantic plains and who were grouped around certain heterodox religious leaders—the prophets of Berghuata—invoking against them the vision of a purer Islam.

The Almoravids of the middle of the eleventh century were really the first to establish a powerful Makhzen. Berber nomads from the Sahara, and from the great 'family' of the Senhaja, they subdued the plains of all the western Maghreb, enlarged Fes, founded the city of Marrakesh and brought tribes of the Senhaja to settle around their capital cities and to provide reliable troops to hold the mountain tribes in check. One still finds traces of these first *gīsh* among the tribes of the Sebu and the Wergha regions as well as the ruins of their forts, like that of Amergo. Masters of Andalusia, the Almoravids found in Spain numerous Arab and Syrian troops whom they recruited into their armies, in which there were also contingents of Christians.

That the Bled el Makhzen at the time of the Almoravids was centred on the plains is demonstrated clearly by the way in which the Almo-hads seized power shortly afterwards. The Almohad movement, led by Ibn Tumert in the early years of the twelfth century, was in effect, despite its religious appearance, a war of independence waged by the settled Berbers of the western Atlas who belonged to the family of the Masmuda. Five great tribes of the region of the Nefis constituted the loyal core which assured success for Ibn Tumert and his successors, the great Sultan 'Abd el Mumen. It took nearly eighty years of war to crush the Almoravid Empire. It is interesting to note that the Almohads rallied to their cause, one after the other, the tribes of the High Atlas, then those of the Central Atlas, then those of the Middle Atlas and of the Rif. For a long while the Almoravids remained complete masters of the plains, where their Christian and Arab cavalry moved freely, and the hardy Berbers of the Atlas did not dare to move down into the Azaghar—the great open plain—where they ran the risk of being surrounded. When they did try they suffered bloody defeats. It was only when they succeeded in blockading the plains region completely that they finally managed to defeat their opponents. The town of Marrakesh, so close to the tribes of the Nefis—for it is visible from the Atlas mountains—fell last of all. This single example demonstrates clearly how the strength of the Almoravids was greatest in the plains and how it was unable to break the resistance of the independent communities of the mountains. Berber society in the west of the Maghreb still remained almost intact.

When the Masmudian Almohads began, in their turn, to become weak as the formerly resilient mountain tribesmen became flabby, as Ibn Khaldun puts it, "from the softness and luxury of civilised living" they recruited Arab tribes (the Hilal from Algeria whom they settled in the plains of the Gharb, the Tadla and Tamesna) to enable them to maintain the number of troops necessary for the conquest of Spain and for the occupation of areas under their nominal control. For the first time since AD 1180 organised Arab tribes had penetrated Morocco. At first they took their place among the humble subjects of the Almohad Empire. Then during the second half of the thirteenth century, when the Almohads, finally exhausted, gave way to the Berber chiefs and nomadic tribes of the Beni Merin, a flood of Ma'qil Arabs from the edges of the Sahara penetrated Morocco and spread via the major routes of the Atlas into the Atlantic plains and along the Muluia river.

The Beni Merin at first established a solid Makhzen, based on the Berber tribes of the plains, the Arabs and the Christian mercenaries. At the time of Ibn Khaldun they were attempting to keep the sedentary tribes of the High Atlas in submission by placing them under the control of great *qāids*, established at the foot of the Atlas. Soon, however, they were struggling in vain to counter both the constant outbreaks of dissidence among the mountain Berbers and the upheaval created in the plains by the Arab invasion. After the end of the fourteenth century the region under Makhzen control was divided by the claims of rival pretenders to the throne.

It was at this point that there began in Morocco a period of complete anarchy. There remained, as a remnant of the central power, only the feeble dynasty of the Beni Wattas, which was confined to the vicinity of Fes. The previously repressed tribes took up their own laws once again, each one regarding itself as an independent 'state'. The only authority that they accepted was that of the religious leaders, who were soon to lead them into holy war against the Portuguese, who were at that time landing along the coasts. Maraboutic states sprang up on all sides out of the ruins of the Makhzen. The establishment of the Sa'dian Empire, itself founded by *shorfa* (the leaders of the holy war) in the middle of the Berber tribes of the Suss, was, as has been demonstrated elsewhere,[13] no more than a brief interlude in the struggle between the marabout lords. At least, however, this ephemeral establishment of a Sa'dian Makhzen—that is, of a strong secular power based on the towns, but which had hardly any effect for over fifty years—left some lasting mark. It brought about a reconcentration of new *gīsh* tribes, composed almost entirely of Arabs, around the towns. From this time onwards Morocco acquired its definitive form. The Ma'qil Arabs, who were soon joined by Arabised Berbers—nomads for the most part—came and set up their tents near the capital cities; it was they who provided troops for the policing and tax-collecting activities of the Makhzen, who provided the Sultan with leaders for his military expeditions, with military officials and with qāids—all forces destined to break up the unity of the Berbers. The Makhzen was thus finally consolidated.

The Filalians began by taking power in a sort of Blitzkrieg. With the assistance of many Berber tribes they reduced the power of the great maraboutic leaders to nothing. Under their assaults Dila disappeared, as did the Berber kingdom of Tazerualt. Moulay Isma'il completed the work by creating a strong black army which he left to provide garrisons for the fortresses built along all the major routes in Morocco. These forts were built not only at stages along the roads of the traditional Bled el Makhzen, but also along the mountain roads at the major points of access to Berber country.

Morocco under Moulay Isma'il was troubled by constant rebellions, led by pretenders to the throne. The Sultan must have spent his whole life on horseback and in battle; but at least it would appear that the areas obstinately rebelling against the imperial authority were reduced by his activities to a few tribes in the highest mountain regions and in the most inaccessible country. The Berbers still champed at the bit.

Moulay Isma'il's successors had a difficult task to accomplish; that was, to rid themselves of this black army left by the great Sultan which, during the reigns of weak monarchs, constituted a major threat. In the reign of Moulay 'Abdullah, during which no fewer than twelve rival Sultans and pretenders were proclaimed in various places, the Bled es Siba (the regions of dissidence and anarchy) expanded greatly so as to encompass a huge area. The three successors of this Sultan—Sidi Mohammed ben 'Abdullah, Moulay Sliman and Moulay 'Abderrahman—tried, with varying degrees of success, to uphold the traditions of the Makhzen during a period of economic decline by executing the frequently troublesome black slaves or by depriving the Arab tribes of their gīsh status when they revolted. They also undertook policing activities in Berber territory, but not without experiencing serious set-backs at times. Particularly damaging to Sherifian prestige was the defeat inflicted upon Moulay Sliman in 1812 by the Ait Umalu—the Berber Senhaja tribes of the Middle Atlas, who were led by the marabout Amhaush. At that period the Bled es Siba extended to the walls of Rabat, Maknes and Fes. The history of the marabouts has left us a colourful account of the revolt of a religious leader during the eighteenth century in the High Atlas near Marrakesh from which one can sense the chafing of the tribes under the temporary yoke imposed by the Makhzen with the help of the Arab tribes of the plains.

The last great Filalian Sultan, Moulay el Hassan, tried to revive the spirit of Moulay Isma'il. He borrowed modern weapons—rifles, cartridges and cannon—from the Christians and managed to re-establish law and order in the Bled el Makhzen (the Arabised areas) and to teach the Berber tribes in many areas, with the exception of the highest mountain regions, a new respect for the Sherifian Makhzen. To achieve this it was necessary for him to spend almost his entire life on *harka* (military expedition). Thus he maintained strict surveillance over the High Atlas and Anti-Atlas and was even able to rally to his side Moha u Hammu, one the leaders of the Zaian and a man who was to become one of the heroes of Berber resistance during the French conquest.

This supreme effort was, however, nullified by the few years of anarchy which followed the death of Moulay el Hassan, and in 1907 when the French landed at Casablanca the Bled es Siba had once again attained its maximum extension.

It is instructive to complete this review of the attempts by the Makhzen to unify 'western Barbary' with a look at the resistance offered to French penetration. If we study the map showing the stages of pacification in Morocco it will enable us to assess the degree of political transformation undergone by Berber society at the beginning of the twentieth century, and also the feeble extent of its unification despite the efforts of the Makhzen over a thousand or so years (see Map 4).

Between 1907 and 1912 it was primarily the Bled el Makhzen—the region controlled by the towns and the imperial government—which was opened up by our troops. The new structure of the Protectorate

E

MAP 4

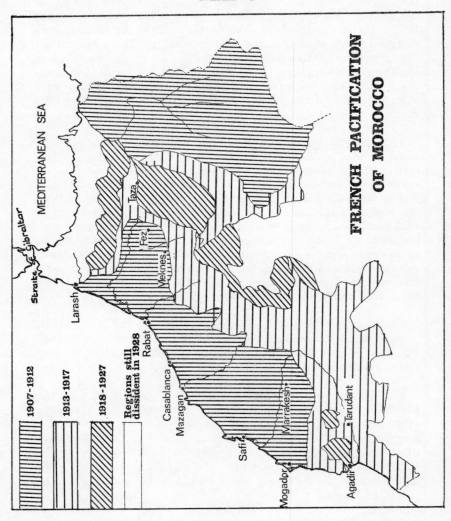

FRENCH PACIFICATION OF MOROCCO

1907-1912

1913-1917

1918-1927

Regions still dissident in 1928

MEDITERRANEAN SEA

Straits of Gibraltar

Larash

Taza

Fez

Meknes

Rabat

Casablanca

Mazagan

Safi

Mogador

Marrakesh

Agadir

Tarudant

very quickly replaced the worn machinery of the old Makhzen as a means of administering the cities and the tribes. From 1912 to 1917 we penetrated all those regions which, while not constituting part of the Bled es Siba proper, had been only periodically controlled by the Arab government; that is, the areas ruled by the great qaids of the Atlas, the plain of the Suss and the nearest tribes of the Middle Atlas —Zemmur, Beni Mgild and Zaian. This is really an intermediary political zone, which corresponds, if you like, to what is, from the point of view of language, a region of bilingualism. In implementing this policy of penetration the tradition of the Makhzen in those areas was sometimes useful to us, but frequently even here force was necessary against certain intractable tribes.

But it was from 1918 onwards that the resistance of the independent and anarchic Berbers made itself most strongly felt; and at that point the influence of the Makhzen was no longer of any assistance. To advance into the Middle Atlas, into the territory of the Beni Warain, and, in the Central Atlas, towards Wawizeght, crude military operations were necessary, as indeed was the constant application of a mixture of force and persuasion to each little mountain tribe. Certain of the dissident groups, like the Ida u Tanan and the Seksawa, agreed to submit only after ten years of gradual and peaceful pressure on all sides. Others were to remain obdurate and hostile until 1934. Finally, there was the extreme violence of the Riffian 'thunder-storm', which is to be explained largely in terms of influences from outside our 'zone', but which also provides a striking demonstration of the political vitality of Berber society and of its preference for a fierce and xenophobic independence, in the isolation of the mountains screened from European and Arab influences.

At the edges of the Sahara the limits of dissidence (since 1927) exclude from the empire only the largely nomadic Berbers of the Central Atlas and of the Saghro. It is interesting to note that, if we except the Moorish tribes of Arab origin, who are still outside our sphere of influence because of the frontier with the Spanish Sahara, the only groups in the Sahara regions that have remained loyal to their tradition of anarchy and freedom all belong to the great and illustrious 'family' of the Senhaja: the transhumants of the Central Atlas, the Ait Yafelman and the Ait Atta of the Sahara. These are the groups which, in 1933 and 1934, provided us with the greatest resistance. The last dissident tribes of the Suss, on the other hand (the already strongly Islamised Shleuh) yielded without a struggle to our powerful forces. France was then able, after thirty-two years' endeavour and thanks to the efforts of our own military and political personnel and to the cooperation of the tribes that submitted to our rule, to achieve the political unification of Morocco, probably for the first time in history. She was determined, at the same time, to integrate the defeated tribes into the Sherifian Empire that the Protectorate had restored and reorganised.

General Characteristics of Berber Society

We shall consider later the political mechanics of the slow break-up of Berber society under the assaults of the Makhzen. Before that, we intend to analyse the structure of the small independent states, their alliances for war and for peacetime, and the political and economic institutions of the independent Berber 'republics'. After that we shall explore the way in which minor secular leaders emerge within the society, how they grow in importance and increase their power, destroying as they do so the very institutions to which they owe their original success. Finally, a description of the conquest of Berber society by the Makhzen, the social and political transformations that this process brings about, and the responses that this in turn provokes, will complete this general analysis of the hidden reality of Moroccan society, of that underlying structure that one looks for in vain in the writings of the Arab historians.

But before launching into this vast subject, we shall attempt to summarise the general features of Berber society—those at least which highlight the contrast between the social organisation of the Berbers and that of the Arab, or Arabised, tribes that have been fully integrated within the empires or Sultanates of North Africa.

What strikes one immediately about Berber society is the almost exclusively rural character of social organisation. If one excludes the small towns of the Mzab, which are the religious cities of a theocratic state, the indigenous sedentary African populations have only villages, hamlets or, quite frequently, just scattered homesteads. Secondly, this rural population is organised in political units (tribes or 'cantons'14) of extremely small dimensions. Several tens of square kilometres and a few hundred homesteads are enough to constitute an independent 'republic'. Whether they are Shleuh, Riffians or Kabyles the Berbers enclose their political, intellectual and economic activities within the bounds of a single high valley, within the strict limits of a canton. From this follows the localism—if we may use such a word— of the Berber existence, which is something that strikes one, not only about their social and political organisation, but also about their technology, their poetry and their folklore, all of which demonstrate minor local peculiarities. At the same time, this love of their native soil encourages among the sedentary Berbers a predilection for autonomy and self-government. The mountain communities will offer untiring resistance to the assaults of the central power.

Among the nomads attachment to the land is replaced by an unrestrained development of the spirit of individual and collective autonomy. As the small social group which constitutes a 'fraction' (the equivalent of a canton among the settled populations) carries with it its own customs and traditions, whether in the inaccessible fastnesses of the mountains or at the edges of the Gharb plain (to which they descend on occasion to flout the authority of a weak Sultan), it is evident that, here again, the Berber way of life remains impenetrable to external influences (or has done for a long while), and maintains its identity in the tents of the elusive herdsmen of the Atlas or the Sahara as well as it does among the remote villages of the Anti-Atlas.

The most pronounced feature then of the Berber ethic will be the existence in every group of a deep conservatism, which is the result of, or possibly the cause of, the existing social fragmentation or atomisation, the deep respect in which they universally hold the customs of their ancestors, and their infinite attachment to their own rituals and symbols, even if the original significance of these has been lost for thousands of years. Secondly, and equally characteristic of Berber society, the fidelity to tradition that is to be found in every little mountain state is associated with an absence of any significant variation in the civilisation that they have thus inherited and conserved. Berber society is, by and large, of an amazing and deep-seated uniformity, from western Egypt to the Atlantic coast and from the Mediterranean to Senegal. The techniques of pottery making, of weaving and of agriculture show strong similarities throughout the Berber areas, despite differences in the mode of existence and in the geographical setting.

The same applies in the sphere of language. The numerous Berber dialects of North Africa possess a remarkable grammatical consistency; at most one can observe certain morphological variations. To distinguish the dialects one from the other one has to rely upon the great phonetic diversity, for it is this poverty-stricken form that local adaptation to a particular region and to a particular type of social life takes. The oral literature is no less monotonous: the same animal tales, the same primitive themes. Just here and there, among the Tuareg, in the Suss and in Kabylia, among groups whose intellectual development has reached its maximum, can one collect a short poem showing some real inspiration: a humble bloom with little real vigour, although not without charm, through which the Berber spirit is best expressed. The music is like the poetry: it boils down to a few nostalgic phrases and is without any great strength. All these features serve to emphasise what is one of the most character-istic aspects of the race: its lack of imagination and its creative poverty.

But if the Berbers are without these gifts of imagination—with which Nature has so liberally endowed the peoples of the Middle East—at least they possess certain sterling qualities which will enable them, it would appear, to achieve pride of place among the peoples of Africa; these are, a robust peasant common sense, a great simplicity of life which often leads them to greed, an often quite genuine modesty and a real willingness to work hard. All these traits serve to distinguish the man of the mountains from the Arab, who will always remain ostentatious, imaginative and a fine orator, even if he is nothing but a ragged herdsman of the Sahara.

Finally, despite its astonishing conservatism, and its loyalty to local traditions, Berber society is not incapable of adaptation and will acquire new forms, often with amazing rapidity. It is true that such adaptation is often only superficial and the changes are restricted to one or two borrowings. (It is for this reason that the Berber language seems to us to be full of ancient Latinisms—names of plants and items of clothing in particular—words of Spanish, Portuguese or English origin, names for weapons or other goods imported since the fifteenth century, and—today—French expressions borrowed from military or administrative language. The influence of Arabic has, of course, been most profound, and many dialects contain between thirty and forty per cent of Arabic words. The Berber language thus constitutes an admirable ethnographic museum in which one may discover the whole history of the race.) It is still too soon, however, to know how far this willingness to adapt that the Berbers show will take them in the future, given the impact of contact with our Western civilisation. One can at least be sure that there will emerge, whether in the sphere of economic activity or in the domain of the intellect, original developments which will merit our attention. While retaining a deep suspicion of changes that are too radical, the Berbers are certainly, today, among those most attracted by the superficial aspects of modern life.

One cannot help but be struck in Morocco by the mediaeval quality of life in the cities. Of all the cities of Islam there are hardly any that have retained their traditional appearance today as well as have those of the far west of the Maghreb. One can still, today, walking through the covered markets of Fes, discover virtually unaltered the capital described in detail by Leo Africanus in the first few years of the sixteenth century. One finds without difficulty the institutions— weakened but not entirely destroyed—of a town that seems to have lain asleep since the time of the Merinids. One may discern, surely, in this amazing preservation the conservative influence exerted by the surrounding countryside upon even the bourgeoisie of the old city.

If we really wish to pursue the game of historical comparisons, however, it is not to our own Middle Ages that we should turn our attention when trying to find analogies with Morocco as a whole. For Morocco remained, until around 1930, very similar to much earlier forms of (Western) society. The Sherifian Empire—the Bled el Makhzen, if you like—demonstrated until then certain features that remind one of the barbarian empires of the West, after the fall of Rome; the Merovingian and Carolingian kingdoms, for example. As for Berber society in the mountains—in the Bled es Siba—in the regions preserved intact in the remote fastnesses of the high peaks, it is more reminiscent of the Western world one or two thousand years before the present than of anything else.

Fifty years ago Masqueray showed, in his fine book, *La Formation des Cités chez les Populations Sédentaires de l'Algérie* how one can discover in the remote hamlets of the Aures, in the small towns of Kabylia and in the religious towns of the Mzab, the successive stages of the development of urban life. He has demonstrated, with many examples, how it is possible to see emerging before our eyes in the Berber areas towns and cities comparable with those which arose four thousand years ago in Greece and Rome.

In the same way, it is perhaps possible to see, in Morocco, the successive developmental stages through which the European tribes of the Bronze Age passed, in the life of the transhumants of the Middle Atlas, or among the mountain folk of the Anti-Atlas, grouped around their collective storehouses. Finally, the minor leaders whom we shall see emerging in the Atlas from among the independent republics will resemble the tyrants who ruled in Greece before the establishment of the empire.

It is therefore possible to investigate today in the Berber areas very ancient forms of social organisation, poorly described in the classical

24 THE BERBERS

texts. This must be the greatest contribution that these antiquated forms, living today before our very eyes, can make to the 'science of peoples', for it makes it possible for us to rediscover the most humble aspects of our own civilisation as it was in its cradle.[15]

NOTES

1 Ibn Khaldun completed the Introduction, or Prolegomena (*muqaddimah*), to his general history (*Kitab al-'Ibar*) in November 1377. It has been described as "the earliest attempt made by any historian to discover a pattern in the changes that occur in man's political and social organisation". See the introduction to *The Muqaddimah* of Ibn Khaldun, edited and introduced by N. J. Dawood, (Bollingen Series, Princeton, 1969). The analysis of Maghreb society developed by Ibn Khaldun has deeply influenced all subsequent sociological and historical work on the subject.

2 The work referred to is *Les Langues du Monde*, edited by A. Meillet and M. Cohen (E. Champion, Paris, 1924).

3 The idea of an 'Arab invasion' by the Beni Hilal in the eleventh century, followed by several other 'waves' of 'Arab invaders' in the next few hundred years, is subscribed to by almost all of the French historians of the colonial period, and certain historians of the post-colonial period; e.g. Abun-Nasr's *A History of the Maghrib* (Cambridge University Press, Cambridge,1971). Such an interpretation has been used to support the conception of an inherent and long-standing opposition and even antagonism between Arabs and Berbers in North Africa. The historical reality of this 'invasion' is open to doubt. For a recent discussion of the question see Yves Lacoste's *Ibn Khaldun: Naissance de l'Histoire Passé du Tiers Monde*, Chapter 4 (Maspero, Paris, 1969).

4 Maurice Le Glay was a novelist and a French officer in the colonial service. In 1912 he was probably the only official in the Protectorate to have any detailed first-hand knowledge of the social organisation of the Middle Atlas tribes.

5 The word derives from the Arabic *jaysh* (army). It refers to those tribes which, in exchange for their formal support of the Sultan and for the provision of troops for the royal army, received the usufruct of land granted them by the Sultan, and which were exempt from all taxes (except for the *zekkat* and the *'ashur*).

6 "By the beginning of the eleventh century AD Islamisation was an accomplished fact", write the authors of the recent *Histoire du Maghreb*. Details of the process of Islamisation in the Maghreb are to be found in Chapters 4, 5 and 6 of *Histoire du Maghreb*, edited by J. Brignon *et al.* (Casablanca, 1967). See also Chapters 4 and 5 of Abun-Nasr's *A History of the Maghrib*.

7 For discussion of the rise of Ibn Tumert and the Almohad reformist movement see *Histoire du Maghreb*, Chapter 8 and *A History of the Maghrib*, Chapter 5.

8 A discussion of modern reformist movements is to be found in Abun-Nasr's *The Salafiyya Movement in Morocco: the religious bases of the Moroccan nationalist movement* (London, 1963); Halstead's *Rebirth of a Nation: the origins and rise of Moroccan nationalism, 1912-1944* (Harvard University Press, Cambridge, 1967); and Pessah Shinar's 'Abd al-Qadar and Abd al-Krim: religious influences on their thought and action', in *Asian and African Studies*, Vol. 1, 1965, pp. 139-174.

9   Probably the best analysis of the social and religious organisation of a small 'maraboutic state', in Montagne's sense, is Gellner's *Saints of the Atlas* (Weidenfeld & Nicolson, London, 1969). Montagne refers explicitly to the marabouts of Ahansal, where Gellner carried out his research. The marabout is a kind of saint, whose sanctity (*baraka*) can be passed on to a follower or descendant.

10   For a fuller and more scholarly discussion of these phenomena see Abun-Nasr's *A History of the Maghrib*, Chapters 4, 5 and 6.

11   The Makhzen (which means literally 'storehouse' or 'treasury') was the name given to the ensemble comprising the Sultan's government and administration. A description of its structure and operation is provided in Chapter 1 of Waterbury's *The Commander of the Faithful*, and also in Lahbabi's *Le Gouvernement Marocain à l'Aube du XXe Siècle* (Rabat, 1958). The nature of the relationship between *makhzen* and *siba* is still a controversial subject; see Gellner's *Saints of the Atlas*, Chapter 1, pp. 22-26.

12   For a detailed discussion of the concept of *baraka* see Westermarck's *Ritual and Belief in Morocco* (2 volumes) (London, 1926) especially Volume I, pp. 35-261. The word can carry a variety of meanings, including 'blessing', 'sanctity', 'abundance', 'gift' and 'power of divine origin'.

13   Montagne refers here, in a footnote, to Cour's *Establissement des Dynasties des Chorfa au Maroc*, n.d., Paris.

14   Montagne uses the term 'canton' to refer to a major segment of a tribe. In so far as members of this segment consider themselves to be members of a political grouping or political unit Montagne's characterisation of such a segment as a 'republic' or a small 'state' is understandable. He argues that such an entity has a sufficient degree of autonomy in most cases for one to be able to consider it as a political system, although he makes it clear that this political system may be, under certain circumstances, a sub-system of a larger inclusive political system equivalent to the tribe or a confederation of tribes. I have thought it best to retain his own term as standard anthropological terms (like 'clan' or 'lineage') are not particularly illuminating in this context.

15   The value of such 'historical comparisons' is questionable to say the least. The idea that particular contemporary societies may in some way 'represent' a past stage in the evolution of society (generally of Western society) and therefore be able to throw light on the structure and organisation of those earlier stages of social evolution has attracted many anthropologists in the past. The idea is clearly attractive, but is fraught with difficulties. A useful discussion of some of these difficulties and of the relationship between evolutionary theories and 'the comparative method' is given in Marvin Harris's *The Rise of Anthropological Theory* (Routledge & Kegan Paul, London, 1969), Chapters 6, 7 and 23.

II

The Social Structure of States and their Alliances in War and Peace

Having analysed how the disintegration of Berber society came about under the three-fold influence of Arabic, Islam and the Makhzen, we must now leave our investigation of the society from the exterior—our investigation of it as it appears from a distance when one restricts oneself to the towns or limits one's horizons to the tribes of the Arabised plains. To understand fully the nature of Berber society it is essential to go beyond the traditional limits of the Sherifian Empire to transport ourselves mentally, with determination, to the heart of the Bled es Siba, among the tribes who have kept their age-old customs intact. We shall restrict ourselves, initially, to an analysis of the structure and the institutions of these social groups, leaving aside for the moment any consideration of changes that they may have undergone.

For the moment, then, we shall attempt only to understand the morphology of the little independent Berber states and to delineate their basic characteristics. Later we shall discuss the alliances which are formed both in times of war and in peace time. This study of Berber society necessitates above all that we disregard the majority of notions we may have about social organisation which derive from experience of our own society.

Method of Study

A complete analysis of Berber society must begin with a detailed investigation of family structure. Among the indigenous populations of the Maghreb the family is markedly patriarchal and agnatic;[1] the importance of this mode of organisation emerges clearly in the model that Berbers have of their kinship structure. Some have suggested that one can discern traces of an earlier matriarchy among certain tribes of the Sahara—namely those whose material culture has remained at a level comparable with that of the peoples of the Neolithic. But even if one accepts the possibility that the matriarchal family among the Tuareg, for example, might have been, in remote antiquity, the normal indigenous form of organisation, it must be pointed out that, throughout almost all of North Africa, even if this was once true, it has now entirely disappeared and has been replaced by an agnatic mode of kinship organisation as strict as that found in early Rome. The study of the customary law of the tribes of the Central Atlas would, we hope, clarify the essential features of Berber family structure. We shall mention here only the misleading way in which the Berbers, like the Arabs, have drawn upon the concepts associated with kinship, which are close and familiar to them, to explain their entire social structure in genealogical terms.[2] To understand the importance of this way of expressing social relationships to the Berbers themselves we have only to open Ibn Khaldun and read what he has to say about the origin of the Berber peoples. "We are not convinced", he writes, "that they are in fact descended from a single ancestor, Mazigh, but they divide themselves into two groups which gave birth to the two groups of the Branès and the Botr. These last produced in their turn a whole brood of offspring, each of whom gave his name to a major Berber grouping. Marriage and the adoption of orphans account for relationships between these groups and one very quickly learns, through studying the history of this human family, the name of the eponymous ancestor of each confederation of tribes and even of each tribe."

All this genealogical romance, though often extremely ingenious, is unfortunately of no value and is revealed as being completely devoid of meaning as soon as one attempts to understand Berber society, not on the basis of ancestral myths but in terms of the reality that may be directly observed. Great Berber families, confederations and tribes, which may appear from a distance to be homogeneous groups of good children descended from fathers and mothers married according to the tradition, are often in reality no more than collections of heterogeneous elements, gathered from the four corners of the horizon and having merely a name in common. This suggestion can be supported in the case of Morocco—as Masqueray observed not long ago for Kabylia and the Aurès—by a study of the origins of different families within the same canton. The names of the ancestors are only labels that are applied to a given social group, labels that are sometimes changed at a particular point in time and which some two or three centuries later find themselves attached to a single hamlet or group of tents as the final piece of historical evidence regarding the evolution of a confederation or a tribe.

There is no other way of analysing Berber society than to maintain an objective and receptive frame of mind, prepared when facing some reality needing investigation to set aside from the outset 'all preconceptions', as Durkheim recommends in his *Rules of Sociological Method*.[3] This is what we shall attempt to achieve in our analysis of the Berber states, confederations, tribes and cantons, not by using historical or genealogical models, but by exploring the very nature of their social institutions.

Social Groups among Sedentary Berbers

A major difficulty results from the fact that the indigenous terminology is very poor and vague, and furthermore it varies from one region to another, and a term used with a certain sense in one place is employed differently in another. In order to avoid confusion we shall fix the terms ourselves, for our own convenience, in the description of each of the social entities that we find superposed in Berber society.

Let us turn first of all to the regions inhabited by sedentary populations: the Anti-Atlas, the Suss, the western High Atlas, the Rif and the Jbala, and also Jurjura Kabylia. (We are, of course, concerned with the natural state of Berber social institutions at a time when our colonial administration had not yet imposed its laws and radically changed the character of local political organisation.) In these regions we find four types, or levels, of social grouping. The smallest, or lowest level, is the *village*—in some regions a federation of three or four hamlets; then comes the *canton*, which is a collection of villages, or else an even greater number of hamlets. Next comes the *tribe*, a federation of several cantons; and finally the *confederation*, formed from a number of tribes, or from many cantons.

The village is most frequently composed, in Berber areas, of several small hamlets in close proximity to each other. Each hamlet is inhabited by a patriarchal family; that is to say, by a group of between ten and fifteen extended families, each one of which regards itself as comprising the descendants of a common ancestor. In reality it is a group of brothers, cousins and second cousins, to whom is added a number of strangers, hired labourers and refugees, who live under the protection of the richest inhabitants and marry the girls of the group; there are also the descendants of slaves freed by their masters. Each patriarchal family has its headman—often the oldest male, or the richest, or else the man most capable of arguing cogently in council (for they discuss matters for a long while, in Berber councils, before reaching agreement).

The group of hamlets which constitutes the village—or a federation of dispersed hamlets, as are seen in the poorer valleys where men are obliged, in order to eke out a living, to maintain their distance from each other—possesses a general council composed of all men of an age to bear arms. This council often meets in the mosque and one can observe that the Friday mosque (that is, the mosque to which forty men must come together to observe the formal prayers), serves as a focal point for the social group. This council, which is called a *jama'a* virtually everywhere, and which is, moreover, quite democratic, rarely has much political power. It meets to supervise the exact distribution of community expenses: the maintenance and repair of the mosque, of the local footpaths and of the irrigation ditches.

Of a quite different importance is the little state that we have termed a canton. It is essential to analyse this entity with the greatest attention, for it is this which truly forms the crucial political unit in all of the settled Berber areas. Its existence can be observed everywhere. It is found in the Anti-Atlas and in the Rif, where it is frequently called a *khums* or *rba'* (a fifth or a quarter of the tribe, although a tribe may sometimes have two, three, seven or eight of these).[4] In the High Atlas it is called *taqbilt*; in Kabylia it is referred to as the *arsh*. In French administrative terminology it is often described as a *fraction* (a fraction of a tribe). We prefer, especially with regard to the settled areas, the term 'canton', which is more expressive and which does not imply that this unit necessarily forms a part of a wider social group. For, in fact, there do exist in the high mountain regions isolated cantons which, on their own, form entirely independent states. Three or four villages, or perhaps ten hamlets—a maximum of four to five hundred extended families in all—are sufficient to constitute an autonomous state. This state possesses a territory with precise boundaries—perhaps enclosing forty to fity square kilometres—within the bounds of a valley. The government is assured by a small oligarchic council—a senate—composed of some ten or so members, who are the headmen of each of the patriarchal families in each hamlet. This senate makes decisions regarding war and peace and, at the same time, it administers the interests of the state. We shall look later at the political institutions of these tiny republics and also at their economic organisation. What concerns us particularly here is the extent and size of the cantons.

What is striking, when one studies one by one the different regions of North Africa inhabited by settled Berber communities is the almost invariable consistency in size and strength of the canton. Its importance appears to be virtually independent of geographical factors. In a large valley, where one might expect the development of an important state of two or three thousand families, one observes that, in fact, there are five or six autonomous cantons. Generally the Berber state fills a high valley, but the reason for this is that Nature provides a ready-made framework in these high regions, tailored to the dimensions of the social group, in the same way that a bee-keeper calculates the size of his hive to suit the average size of the swarms that he can capture. This is so true that we can see, if we study the history of these cantons through the local traditions, reconstructing it backwards over three or four generations, that prosperous and densely populated cantons divide spontaneously into two. The more powerful villages succeed in attaching weaker villages to their initial group and form a new canton. But the canton never exceeds eight hundred extended families, it divides into two or three segments when it has grown above the limits laid down according to some hidden law—which is probably determined by the inability of the relatively weak councils to extend their authority over more than a certain number of families. One could compare this constancy of the Berber political unit with that of certain single-cell species in the world of the lower forms of life, which reproduce by division.

Whatever may be the fundamental causes of this structure, there can be no doubt that the political institutions play a major role in determining the social organisation of these cantons.[5] In the High Atlas the canton has a president, elected for a year, a common budget and a special set of precepts within the customary law laying down the punishment to be exacted for crimes and transgressions. In the Rif and Jbala it sometimes has a flag and often a traditional leader. In Kabylia, at the time of the French conquest, the *arsh* (the local equivalent of the canton) had a president (*amin*) as well as a council. After Jurjura lost its independence and the French reorganised the area in a somewhat arbitrary manner into 'duars' and 'communes', the arsh disappeared and it is in the village—a particularly dense and active section of society—that Berber social organisation has been concentrated. The reports of early travellers in Kabylia, however, are quite clear on this point: the arsh—the major political unit of the area—had at that time (around 1855) the same importance that the canton has retained in the settled parts of Morocco up until the present day.

Above the canton is the tribe. It is here that the difficulties begin as far as direct observation is concerned. The characteristics of the higher levels (tribe and confederation) are as difficult to pin down for analysis as those of the canton are easy. The tribe is really a federation of cantons, but in certain regions this federation exists only *potentially* and each autonomous republic normally lives without any particular involvement with its neighbours. It requires an outside threat for all the cantons—or, in other words, every *khums* or *rba*—to send their own council members to an agreed place to consider the problem. Even then, they are not always able to reach an agreement. In the High Atlas, the Suss and Rif, for example, they cannot even manage to select a single overall leader, even when conflict with the Makhzen is imminent. Each one defends its own frontiers as it wishes. In Kabylia, we are told, there were amins of whole tribes and even of confederations, elected as a kind of president for the duration of military operations, in the period before European intervention. What contributes most generally to the establishment of a degree of unity within the tribe is the existence of some common body of customary law regarding homicide and theft; also important is the belief—purely fictional—in a common origin, or the existence of natural geographical boundaries; or else again, the fact that the cantons have a mosque or a market in common. Occasionally the force that welds the tribe together is a hatred shared by all its cantons for a neighbouring tribe. Finally, it is also sometimes the existence of an unusual form of internal organisation, baffling to our logical minds. A tribe is, for instance, composed of four cantons; in this case the wider group will comprise two opposed segments—two against two. If the tribe has six cantons the two segments will be three against three. Thus one can suggest that when one takes up a dispute the forces tend to be equally matched on either side and the struggle may be continued without risk of overwhelming defeat. It is possible, in short, to kill each other in open warfare without incurring irreparable losses and without being forced to call in allies from outside.[6]

The confederation is even more difficult to define than the tribe. It is a collection of four or five, or sometimes as many as ten to twelve, tribes, or else of forty or fifty cantons, either autonomous or themselves grouped into tribes. With the exception of Kabylia (and even there it is rare) the confederation never has an elected leader, at least not among the sedentary populations. Occasionally it may have a sanctuary which all members of the confederation will regard as their own. One might suggest that it does not become aware of its own identity until it is controlled by a single leader, whether one who has seized power of his own accord or one imposed by the Makhzen; or else again, in periods of great conflict when large numbers of people come into direct confrontation, as occurs after an invasion. Sometimes, under such circumstances, there develops within the confederation a hierarchy or some kind of military organisation among the constituent tribes, according to which the different groups move away or advance into battle on the basis of a well-defined system known to all. Sometimes an artificial confederation is formed on a geographical basis, usually in order to oppose the forces of the Makhzen; that of the Ida u Tanan, situated to the north of Agadir at the extreme end of the Atlas range, is the best example of this. The members of the confederation may, after centuries of activity, acquire a sort of historical memory of the glorious deeds accomplished together; but these memories generally disappear quite quickly and after a few generations there remains only an empty framework within which everyone does as he wishes. The name may last as a sort of label, and this may be retained for a very long period, for in Berber society everything is always retained, even when it no longer has any meaning. There are, however (and the writings of the historians confirm this), cases where the name has retained some significance although the original confederation has long since disappeared. In the High Atlas, for instance, certain confederations within the great Masmudian 'family' who took part in the great Almohad movement of the twelfth century, have not endured. The Genfisa, for example, or the Hintata, can no longer be identified on the ground; but, on the other hand, when we possess the list of the cantons which made up these confederations of the twelfth century it is possible to identify the component parts of these major groupings within the same area today, in between forty and fifty per cent of cases. Fine proof of the conservatism of these parent cells of the Berber body social! These cells are, of course, the small autonomous republics, the tiny states formed by a single canton which, actually by virtue of their small size, manage to avoid the destructive action of time.

This smallness, this constancy and this vitality of the basic Berber state—which is the canton—are social facts which have extremely important implications for the history of North Africa, implications whose significance has not always been fully appreciated. It is upon this very limited stage, for the most part, that the various processes which constitute the basic elements of any political drama in the Maghreb are played out. Here we observe the birth and rise to power of leaders, the competition between leaders and their relations with the mass of the people, here we may study the pressures of the Makhzen and the outbreaks of rebellion. It is easy to understand, on realising the size of these states, what limited conceptions can stir the

F

hearts of council members in these mountain republics whose horizon is drawn by the ridges which surround their valley.

Two things follow from this. First of all (and something that was mentioned at the beginning of this study) the fundamental conservatism of Berber society, preserved by the small dimensions of these states from outside influences. (This attachment to traditions will produce an almost invincible form of resistance as long as the overall structure of Berber society remains intact.) Second, the fragmentation of the society makes it necessary to use force in order to break the framework of these anarchic states. Nothing of significance can emerge from this mosaic of tribes as long as the frontiers have not been obliterated. It is this task to which, on occasion, secular leaders emerging from the very heart of such mountain republics have turned their efforts in an attempt to found chiefdoms, kingdoms and empires by force.

Let us now look, for comparison, at the structure of those small states formed, whether in central Morocco, the Sahara or in the Aures, by Berber transhumants and nomads. Here again we can identify a number of superposed groupings. The important ones are: the group of *duars* that we can call the *sub-fraction*, the *fraction*, which is frequently composed of two or three sub-fractions, the *tribe*, which comprises several fractions (four or five at least), and the *confederation* of several tribes.

The mobility of the constituent elements—for the duars grow or decrease in size (i.e. the number of tents) according to the season or else depending upon local politics and the question of security—makes it impossible to define the structure of the various states with the same accuracy as was possible for the sedentary groups. There are, however, several features of the social morphology of pastoral communities which may be easily identified. Firstly, the extreme individualism of the warriors, which is explained well enough by the conditions under which they live. Despite the existence of a strongly patriarchal kinship structure, every male of the age to bear arms manages, in pastoral society, to free himself from a large number of constraints, and he appears, for this reason, as an even greater individualist than his sedentary compatriot.

But if the lower level (the sub-fraction) often seems to be devoid of precise features, the fraction, which corresponds at least in dimension to the canton of the settled communities, has a quite remarkable vitality. The fraction is a political and fighting unit; it has its council, comprising the heads of the important families, and it nominates the war leader, who is referred to by the term widely known throughout the Central Atlas: *amghar n-tuga* (leader with a tuft of grass). The leader is given this name after one of the rituals which accompany his accession to power. When he is elected, a tuft of grass (couch grass or sometimes sweet basil) is inserted in the cotton band or hair-cord with which he binds his head, and his clothes are rubbed with a handful of grass. The fraction often possesses communal land, acquired by conquest, and each of its members is considered to have potential rights in this land and also a right of redemption on the land possessed by other adult males. It is sometimes even the case that the identity of the fraction is stressed by the existence of specific female tattoos, which are registered, like manufacturers' marks or marks of owner-ship, at the *zawia* or religious sanctuary.[7]

The tribe has no well defined distinguishing features among pastoralists, any more than it has among the settled agriculturalists. Occasionally it may have a temporary war leader, but it rarely has institutions which incorporate all its constituent fractions. The confederation, on the other hand, which is such a loosely structured grouping among the sedentary populations, has here a considerable importance. This should probably be seen as an unconscious reaction against the dispersal of tentholds within the duars and the sub-fractions. It is also a consequence of a state of more or less permanent conflict, which is prevalent among populations constantly on the move. Even if the confederation has, strictly speaking, no specific institutions other than a uniform body of customary law by which all members are bound, its solidarity is assured by the strength of the powerful feelings of unity and mutual obligation which emerge in times of conflict. Our military officers in the Middle Atlas have recognised this for a long time past. "When you wish to pacify them", Maurice Le Glay makes one of his heroes say in a novel, "you will find before you only a scatter of humanity. You have to chase after each tent in order to talk to the head of each small family, and to establish any sort of control over them at all requires years. If you face them in battle though they fall upon you all at once and in vast numbers, and you wonder how you can possibly extricate yourself."

If one compares the structure of the Berber states among the pastoralists with those of the settled tribes, one is quite soon led to suggest an hypothesis to account for certain peculiar features observed among the latter. It is not unreasonable to suppose that the majority of Berber groups who are now settled originally (at some very early period) lived in tents and took possession of the country, in much the same way as do today the Berber and Arab transhumants of central Morocco, who sweep in successive waves from the desert as far north-west as the plains of the Gharb. We shall see below how one may perhaps discover, even among long-settled populations, survivals of this wandering life in the form of collective storehouses. One is forced to conclude that sedentarisation—the settlement of nomadic groups —has been responsible for the gradual alteration of their social structure.

The fraction of the transhumants, united on occasion by the conquest of a particular area, brought together also perhaps by virtue of some sort of indefinable social instinct, and which values its political institutions, is gradually replaced by the canton. In the canton, by contrast, it is the land which holds the individual and takes him to its breast. It is no longer kinship that provides the links between individuals. The importance of the elementary social group thus never ceases to grow as the Berbers establish themselves permanently in a high valley or on a plateau whose borders they are prepared to defend. At the same time, the higher levels atrophy and become, as we have already noted, no more than empty frameworks among the sedentary populations. The present provides no explana-tion for their existence; it is to the past that we must turn if we seek to understand their significance. They are, it would seem, the external manifestations (the skeletons) of those great hordes of invaders who arrived thousands of years ago and overran the mountain regions. To bring them back to life again for a short while requires a great clash between peoples or a violent attack by the Makhzen, for this revives once more within their frames the spirit of unity that time has gradually destroyed. As the process of sedentarisation took place in the Berber areas there came about, at the same time, a sort of reconstitution of the society from within. A reconstitution which, with the slowness characteristic of social change in Morocco, is still at a very preliminary stage for, without exception, the independent mountain communities never manage to extend their horizon beyond that of a canton of two thousand inhabitants.

The Alliances

Within Berber society there exist forms of alliance between groups. (In order to understand fully their nature and their significance we must once again lay aside those concepts that are familiar to us and refuse to call upon 'logic', 'utility' or 'common sense' to explain the facts; instead we must observe the facts as they are and leave the explanation until later.) We are referring here to the institutions of *leff* and *soff*, which are widespread throughout Berber society.[8]

Let us consider first of all the situation existing in the peak districts of the High Atlas, to the south of Marrakesh, in the region of the Nefis and the Seksawa which was the cradle of the Almohad movement. We observe that there alliances are formed between the autonomous mountain cantons which result in the development of two great opposed blocs, which are termed leffs.

When a canton enters into a state of war with one of its neighbours it receives assistance from the next canton but one, and step by step there develops a sort of vast political chequer-board in two colours. These blocs are very stable and it is considered a great dishonour if a canton changes allegiance. We know from the history of the marabouts of the High Atlas that they have hardly changed at all, at least during the last one hundred and fifty years. Among the Seksawa the leff of the Indhertit has been opposed to that of the Imsifern for generations. A little to the east, in the valley of the Nefis, the Ait Atman oppose the Ait Iraten, and the valley occupied as it is from its head to its foot by six or seven cantons belonging to one or other of the coalition groups, may thus become involved in an upheaval extending over a considerable distance when conflict breaks out, even though the original dispute might have involved no more than a couple of villages. Further to the east again the two blocs have other names, but despite the multiplicity of names there are in reality only two alliances which divide all the mountain cantons, over an area of some eighty kilometres wide by one hundred and fifty long, into two sections.

These leffs are, above all, alliances in times of war, which involve reciprocal obligations of loyalty between all the cantons of the same bloc. They may also, however, be peacetime coalitions, and it is true that economic relations are frequently established by preference with states belonging to the same political alliance. In the same way the political intrigues which permeate the region are themselves affected by the leff allegiances of canton leaders. Not long ago, loyalty to one's leff alliance and the idea of mutual assistance between 'leff-brothers' was a strict, and almost sacred, obligation among the mountain folk of the High Atlas, especially in the high valleys. It was re-emphasised each year in major festivals during which war dances renewed the feelings of solidarity held by every member of the alliance. Today, the growing power of the great qaids has radically altered the whole institution (of leffs) and it has virtually disappeared from the northern regions of the great mountain range, especially in the foothills. Fifty years ago, however, when internal warfare broke out between two blocs it was not unusual to find warriors coming from areas two or three days' march away to support their leff-brothers, whom they did not even know. In the same way, when anarchy developed within a canton to a dangerous extent, and threatened to weaken the leff, allies from neighbouring cantons came to occupy the warring villages and to impose peace upon the disputants.

There is no use in questioning the Berbers of the High Atlas about the origin of this curious institution which served to maintain a balance of power between cantons. They only reply that their forefathers have always respected this tradition and that it has been so since the time of their ancestors' ancestors. The institution appears so normal to them in fact that they imagine that we also, the French and other Europeans, live in tribes divided into leffs, and our constant wars in which Germany opposes France and England tend to confirm them in this belief. It is such a basic part of social life that they do not even discuss it.

If one studies Berber society in other parts of North Africa one soon realises that the institution of leffs, although showing certain variations from place to place, is a virtually ubiquitous phenomenon. In the Anti-Atlas there are two great opposed blocs—the Igezulen and the Ahoggwa u Isuqtan. The leff of the Igezulen claims to be the noble leff; that of the Ahoggwa is not particularly honourable—no one quite knows why—and few are proud to say that they belong to it (which does not make the work of the sociologist any easier). Sometimes they suggest, as an explanation for the existence of the two leffs, that the Igezulen are *shorfa*—people of noble descent who brought Islam from the Sahara—while the Ahoggwa are descendants of the indigenous population of the region—pagans and possibly even Jews. It should be mentioned that in the Anti-Atlas the elements which make up the political chequer-board resulting from the opposition of the two leffs are not cantons, as in the High Atlas, but whole tribes. Often they are groupings of great importance. For example, almost all of the confederation of the Ida Ultit—historically best known for the assistance they gave the Berber chiefs of Tazerualt—belong to the Igezulen leff. The stability of leffs in the Anti-Atlas, on the other hand, is by no means complete, and we know that fifty years (or maybe a century) ago one or two tribes of the plains changed allegiance. Finally, in the oasis regions, where the population is more mixed, the leffs divide by villages, or even occasionally by hamlets, depending on the origins of those who had come down from the mountains to establish themselves on the uncultivated land as colonisers.

In the Jbala and the Rif the political chequer-board is made up of tribes, or even of confederations, as it was in the Anti-Atlas. The two blocs carry the names of the two great Berber 'families' who came into conflict in the past: the Ghomara, who are the most ancient of the settled populations, and the Senhaja, who were invaders, coming probably from the Sahara during the first centuries of the Muslim period. The similarity between this situation and that prevailing in the Suss is remarkable. In the case of the Jbala and the Rif each bloc is seen today less as a homogeneous ethnic group than as a straight-forward political coalition. It is an 'alam, as they say (a flag); and, in fact, it is not uncommon to find a small tribe slipping from one banner to another when it is in its interest to place itself under the protective standard of a powerful neighbouring tribe. Such realign-ments are much more common here than in the south. What gives a unique flavour to the leffs of the north of Morocco is the curious list of names, reminiscent of totemic emblems, which applies to the various tribes. This is the list of Bu Tiur, according to which the Ghomara tribes have the names of animals that one may eat, while those of the Senhaja have the names of animals that one is not permitted to eat. Again, it is suggested that the Ghomara tribes have the names of birds, and those of the Senhaja the names of mammals, while groups of mixed origin have names of fish. These animal names are not confined to the Jbala; one also finds them in the Anti-Atlas, but in the south of Morocco they are not related to the division into leffs.

We should add, so as to avoid misconceptions, that the leffs in the north of Morocco are survivals from previous periods rather than effective institutions today, at least in the central and eastern Rif. While the organisation of leff alliances has often conditioned tribal politics in the High Atlas and the Anti-Atlas to a considerable extent, even in the last decades, and while the origin and subsequent rise to power of political leaders in those areas appears to be closely related to the existing patterns of war alliances, it seems that in the Rif, on the other hand, the two great blocs (the two 'alams) have been part of past history for more than fifty years. They have remained effective into the twentieth century only in the region between Wezzan, Tetuan, Tangier and Larash. We should also point out that in every region these are internal divisions which, although running deep, cease to operate in Berber areas instantaneously as soon as foreigners —whether these be the Sultan, Arabs or even French and Spanish military expeditions—attempt to penetrate into the mountains. They are institutions which are significant only within Berber society.

We should conclude these remarks on the Berber leffs in Morocco with a comment on those which have been identified in Kabylia, where they have been known for a long while under the name of *soffs*. The cleavage into two blocs of allies is found throughout Jurjura Kabylia; here the soffs comprise neither tribes nor cantons, but villages and often even segments of villages. In the various important confederations of Kabylia there are soffs which extend over considerable areas and which divide cantons and villages into two sections. They are referred to as the 'upper soff' and 'lower soff', or the 'soff of the people from the east' and 'soff of the people from the west', and so on, although these geographical references have no precise significance. Any dispute which breaks out and which threatens to result in armed conflict provokes a response from the two soffs, and each recruits fighting-men from within its own party. There are individuals who shift allegiance from one soff to another for reasons of self-interest.

In the republics of Kabylia before 1871 the president of the small village council (*amin*) was often chosen from one of the soffs, while the *ukil*, responsible for the keeping of accounts, belonged necessarily to the other. Today political disputes within a region spread freely along the lines of cleavage provided by the two traditional alliances, in the same way as electoral rivalries in Corsica frequently follow the lines of ancient family quarrels. The institution of leffs also occurs in other parts of Morocco, in the areas traditionally controlled by the Makhzen; and here, despite certain differences and alterations, the fundamental picture is essentially the same. It would seem that here we have a survival of the indigenous traditions of the country, which continue to exist despite the general destruction of the political structure.

Before trying to explain how these political and ethnic alliances—which maintain a sort of natural equilibrium throughout Berber society, and which also are probably among the most powerful forces for the maintenance of Berber conservatism—could be generated, it is necessary to say a few words about the way in which the alliances show certain differences among transhumants and nomads.

We have remarked earlier upon the individualist tendencies of each family-head in a group of nomadic Berbers and, as a sort of reaction, the feelings of solidarity between members of the higher segments which form the confederation. In time of war this two-sided sentiment operates in the following manner. If a dispute breaks out between two families within the same group each builds up its leff so that a balance is established between close kinsmen on both sides. If they are people from two different duars who come to blows they call, if necessary, upon reinforcements from outside, so that here too an equilibrium of forces is established. The same obtains if the conflict is between fractions of tribes, or even between confederations. It is even possible—and this has been seen to happen several times in the last few centuries in northern Morocco—for the conflict to develop to the extent that all the Arabs of the Gharb plain find themselves ranged against the combined Berbers of the Middle Atlas. The principle ensures that equal numbers of combatants are arrayed on either side without any particular consideration for the actual position of tribes on the ground. It is only when a social group—say, a confederation—settles because it finds itself virtually surrounded by sedentary tribes, for instance, and has no further access to grazing in the mountains, that one observes the development of the political chequer-board of opposed factions, each one with its own land to defend.

Historical Conjecture

We may now attempt to pull all the data presented so far together to formulate a hypothesis which is supported to a satisfactory degree by numerous direct observations and a certain number of historical accounts. When the Berbers were still nomads they clashed in great numbers and came to feel an extremely powerful sense of ethnic kinship, which was represented in their minds by the idea of the confederation. This sentiment of close brotherhood, which was reinforced by ties of adoption, provided a considerable cohesion for any group of invaders, despite the anarchic tendencies of the race. When a horde of invaders—the Senhaja, for example, on their arrival in the Rif—came into contact with populations that had been long settled in a particular region, the conflict took on a purely ethnic appearance at the outset. Then, little by little, the new arrivals established themselves in their turn and the wars which took place after that time resulted in the gradual emergence of two blocs. Small tribes shifted their allegiance from one bloc to another and thus there developed in the north of Morocco, over a period of perhaps eight centuries, a chequer-board whose different 'squares' were tribes or confederations.

The Anti-Atlas with its two leffs—the Igezulen and the Isuqtan u Ahoggwa—provides us with an analogous situation. In the High Atlas, a region of longer settled and more stable populations, we are dealing with leffs that are still more fragmented. The process of disintegration here reached even the smallest political units, the cantons. It is noticeable, at the same time, that the names of the coalitions here are no more than the names of tribes or ancient fractions: Imsifern, Indghertit, Ait Atman, and so on. Finally, in Kabylia, where the disintegration continues, it is the village which is divided into two. In this last region we can see the final stages of a process that has probably been taking place for several thousand years.

Let us set this overall picture that we have just painted beside that of the reconstitution from within of confederations and, among the settled populations, of tribes, and that of the structure of the canton within the larger states, tribes and confederations that are frameworks for social organisation which date from that far-off period of invasions, and we shall have some idea of the developments that can take place within Berber society.

These changes are extremely slow. In this deeply traditionalist environment, where the rituals of ancient religions are retained indefinietly without utility or meaning, for ten or more centuries, we can nevertheless identify the emergence of spontaneous transformations. But as these changes cannot, by virtue of their slowness, be directly observed, we have no other means of studying their course than to compare the various groups of Berbers presently scattered throughout North Africa. To explain the gradual formation of leffs we have to bring together for comparison information from those of Kabylia, those of the Masmuda of the Atlas, of the Shleuh of the Anti-Atlas and those from the Rif and Jbala. One could, as we shall see shortly, analyse many other institutions by making such multiple comparisons. This mode of investigation is particularly fruitful in the Berber regions.

The reason for this is that the peoples scattered throughout the various regions of North Africa all evolved very slowly, but at different speeds nevertheless. There are those who remained for the longest period in the desert, like the Tuareg, the Aurasians and the Senhaja of the Moroccan Central Atlas, who remain even today in the grip of a social structure like that of the Neolithic period. Others, like the Kabyles of Jurjura and the people of the Mzab, have almost reached the stage of development attained by other rural populations of the Mediterranean during the Roman period. Thus the various Berber regions offer a wonderful field of research for sociologists and ethnographers. Here, better than in our own civilisation, agitated and overwhelmed by unceasing progress as it is, we may grasp the interplay of the multiple forces acting upon the lives of men, which push them slowly, without their being aware of it, towards ends that they would not recognise, and which lead them to found cities and states at the cost of infinite effort and of conflicts without number. From the peaks of the Atlas mountains we may also meditate upon a past that books cannot describe and which must have been somewhat like our own prehistory.

NOTES

1   Montagne uses 'la famille' in three senses. In the first place it refers to a major socio-linguistic grouping, like the Senhaja; secondly, it refers to the lineage or patrilineal descent group, and finally, it is also used to mean just the extended, or even the nuclear, family. The context usually makes it clear which meaning is intended, but I have simplified the situation by placing 'family' (a socio-linguistic grouping) between single inverted commas wherever it appears. The significant 'family' in Montagne's discussion of local political organisation is what he refers to as 'the patriarchal family', which I should prefer to call the 'patrilineal descent group' or simply the 'patrilineage'. Where Montagne speaks of 'patriarchy' and 'matriarchy' modern social anthropology would use the terms 'patrilineal descent' and 'matrilineal descent'. 'Agnatic' descent is equivalent to 'patrilineal descent'; in a society utilising this principle of social organisation a man belongs to his father's group whereas, in a society with matrilineal descent he belongs to the group of his mother's brother. For further discussion of these and related concepts see Fox's book, *Kinship and Marriage*.
2   The social structure may be expressed in a 'kinship idiom', so that all past and present relationships between individuals or between groups can be explained, and justified, in terms of genealogical links and contemporary kinship relations. For a discussion of the relationship between 'folk models' of society based upon genealogical concepts and 'sociological models'; see Peters' article on 'Some structural aspects of the feud among the camel-herding Bedouin of Cyrenaica', in *Africa*, Vol. XXXVII, No. 3, 1967. See also, in this connection, two works by Evans-Pritchard, *The Nuer* and *The Sanusi of Cyrenaica*; and an article by Laura Bohannan: 'A genealogical charter' in *Africa*, 1952.
3   The influence of Durkheim on the French colonial sociologists and historians was as strong as it was on French scholars in the metropolitan country and began to have a significant impact as early as the 1890's. The influence was not all one way, however, and we find several references to the work of Hanoteau, Letourneux and Masqueray in Algeria in *The Division of Labour in Society*. See also Bottomore's *Sociology: a guide to problems and literature*, Chapter 2, for a commentary on Durkheim and sociological theory.
4   The precise relationship between the tribal segment that Montagne calls the canton and the *khums* or *rbaʿ* is not always clear. In many cases they are evidently different terms used for similar or identical segments of the tribe, but in the central Rif at least it would appear that the *khums* is something different from the 'canton'. See Hart's 'Segmentary systems and the role of the "five fifths" in tribal Morocco', in *Revue de l'Occident Musulman et de la Méditerranée*, No. 3, 1er trimestre, 1967.
5   When Montagne refers to 'political institutions' he is concerned primarily with the structure and organisation of the canton (and tribal) councils, and there-

44 THE BERBERS

fore with what might be termed 'government' or 'administration' as much as with politics.

6 The development of two opposed factions in intra-tribal, and even in inter-tribal, conflict is a theme to which Montagne returns later (p. 62) and which is discussed briefly in my Introduction.

7 *Zawia*—usually translated as 'lodge'—is the place where the marabouts, or saints, live and work, or alternatively it is the institution itself: the collectivity of saints.

8 The importance of these alliances and political coalitions has been widely recognised by students of North African society but scholars differ in their understanding of the structure and organisation of these crucial social phenomena. For some discussion see: Gellner, *Saints of the Atlas*, pp. 64-68; Hart's forthcoming book on the Ait Waryaghel of the central Rif; and Waterbury, *The Commander of the Faithful*, pp. 61-80.

III

Political and Economic Organisation

One of the most characteristic features of Berber social organisation is the existence of a hierarchy of small states, from the canton or the fraction up to the tribe or confederation; another is the structure of alliances which enables them, by the process of coalition and opposition, to form blocs of a very particular kind. In order to complete the synchronic picture of the traditional and static Berber society we must now describe their political institutions and economic organisation.

We have drawn attention to the extreme uniformity of Berber society, whose heritage of primitive culture (which is poor enough, it is true) is found again and again in a virtually identical form throughout North Africa, and which reveals only minor variations from region to region. This fundamental unity of Berber culture, so evident in the realm of language, thought and technology, is no less apparent in that of political organisation.

In all those regions where the indigenous populations of North Africa have maintained their independence and their own institutions intact and beyond the reach of the Makhzen or the Arab or Turkish Beyliks the most usual and most durable form of political organisation, and that to which they hasten to return as soon as they have left it for a while, is that of the 'republican regime'. We use this term 'republic' with some reluctance to refer to the most stable form of government in Berber society, lacking any more suitable word. We do not mean to imply by this the kind of government which requires the cooperation and participation of the masses. If it may be termed a republic, then it is truly an oligarchy. To be more precise the Berber style of government is anarchic; that is to say, it lacks an overall leader or chief. Nevertheless it attempts to ensure an equitable distribution of the benefits and the responsibilities of power between the representatives of the major patriarchal families of the region. This *ordered anarchy*,[1] in which all Berbers take delight, is virtually never able to control the organisation of a state of any importance, and it would seem that the entire fund of political wisdom possessed by any mountain group is exhausted by the establishment of a republic whose territory is that of a canton.

The Canton Republic

We have already described the amazing consistency in canton size among the settled Berbers of North Africa. Between two hundred and four hundred families, and between forty and fifty square kilometres of territory are sufficient everywhere to constitute the basis of a state.

The heads of the patriarchal families, each of which inhabits a hamlet or a part of a village, meet in a single assembly which forms the council of the Berber republic. It is probably true that the form of political organisation has at least some effect on the size of the state itself. The extent of the canton will be roughly determined by the necessity for the council of notables to be able to meet, discuss and disperse again within the space of a day.

In fact the council of a canton is an extremely active form of government and its meetings are frequent. Let us look first at the way in which it regulates the affairs of the state and controls political activity in the western High Atlas. That done, it will be enough to make comparisons between the situation found there and the situation as it exists in the republics of the Rif and of Kabylia, in order to obtain a precise understanding of what is, from the Berber point of view, the ideal form of government.

Throughout much of the High Atlas, fifty years ago, before the emergence of the great qaids and the associated disruption of earlier forms of political organisation, the majority of cantons were ruled by a council of notables[2] presided over by a leader elected for a year at a time. These notables are called *inflas** in the south of Morocco, and

* This term *inflas* (sing. *anflus*), which derives from the Berber root FLS (to have confidence), and whose meaning corresponds roughly to that of the Arabic *umana* (sing. *amin*), once had, perhaps, connotations of magical power. There are, as Doutté has suggested for a long time, persons renowned for their *baraka*, and who precede others, setting themselves in the forefront on important social occasions. They are also called *inflas el khir*. In the councils of notables one occasionally finds men who have been asked to sit on the council by virtue of their possession of benign powers. These men are called *mbarkin*.

sometimes also *ait arbaʿin*.* This council meets at the home of one of its members who has a guest-room, or alternatively at the mosque, in the sanctuary, or at some acceptable place in the open air under a tree or on the cleared space used for threshing. It discusses, endlessly, all the problems of local current affairs: the state of the footpaths and of the irrigation ditches; the right time for the nut harvest or for harvesting proper, or else for the departure to new pastures; external policies, relations with neighbouring republics, and, above all else, the question of the arbitration of disputes between citizens of the republic and the punishment of crimes and offences. In all the decisions that it takes the council draws its inspiration from the known interests of the canton, but also, and especially, from the dictates of tradition.

For the execution of its decisions the council nominates, generally by lottery, or according to some other principle determined by local custom, a president who will act as such for a year. This is the *moqaddem*.† Constitutional measures are taken to control his actions and above all to ensure that he does not prolong his stay in office beyond the fixed term. Sometimes he is reappointed for a further year, if his period of 'government' has been successful, but never more, for the Berber councils are highly suspicious and are always fearful that a tyrant may arise. The moqaddem must hold the balance on behalf of all the citizens and mediate the struggle, that is frequently very bitter, between the heads of powerful families. It is rare that a council does not comprise two factions, ever ready to quarrel between themselves, and often in fact there are only three or four men of real importance, and in such cases the moqaddem is a puppet of one of them.

The major problem in the Berber republic is the distribution of the benefits of office. When the moqaddem takes up his office he often produces a list of rules of office which, if infringed by him during his period in power, may be upheld by the exaction of previously determined fines. It is a sort of pledge, valid for a year, which is consigned to writing and which, after the list of penalties obtaining, bears the names of all those notables present. The fines, if exacted, go to swell the common fund of the canton, which is also sometimes fed

* *Ait arbaʿin*—the Forty. This term is very widely found among Berber groups throughout the Maghreb. In many regions one finds a representative body of ten notables sitting in the tribal council. The *ait arbaʿin* may have originally been a body composed of four groups of ten members, representing the members of the whole tribe. At the level of the canton the *ait arbaʿin* very rarely number as many as forty.

† An Arabic word meaning: 'one whom one places before oneself'.

by more general contributions. This fund serves to subvent expenses incurred by offering hospitality, or other minor expenses of government. The remainder, however, is often shared out. The proportion received provides a means of assessing the relative power of the moqaddem, the ordinary member of the council and the common citizen of the canton, or 'tribe' as it is usually called. The general rule is to divide the amount into three equal parts, but if the moqaddem becomes really powerful it is not unusual for him to take the share of the common people for himself; in other cases, however, it is the council as a whole which 'eats' the share of the rest of the 'tribe'. There is no surer way of estimating the power of a leader or notable than to know what he receives from the distribution of the fines' fund.

One can hardly credit the greed and rapacity of the notables and the moqaddem. The council may, for example, discuss the problem of how to divide three centimes into seventeen for three or four hours; or else they may quarrel among themselves because some passing guest has been invited to share the meal that is offered to the notables by a criminal as a form of reparation and as a peace-offering. In this case each diner calculates that he has been deprived of a small portion of his own share because the guest has eaten more than three mouthfuls of the dish provided.

There are certain regions—in the Suss and the rebellious Anti-Atlas, for example—where no moqaddem is appointed for fear of the rise of a dictator. The centralisation of the state is less strong in those parts. There the council meets in the canton and if, for example, a crime has been committed the culprit is made to pay a fine, divisible into twelve of fifteen parts, which is shared out immediately among the notables, for in those regions there is no central fund. After this distribution has taken place those heads of families who are allies of the culprit will secretly return to him what he paid them, on condition that he agrees to do the same for them when necessary. Because of this unwillingness to risk the emergence of a tyrant the canton is constantly fraught with internal discord and anarchy.

In other tribes, as among the Ida u Tanan, at the extreme head of the Atlas, or in the Anti-Atlas among the Ida Ultit, there is no moqaddem either, and each canton is autonomous. But here, in order to inhibit the development of anarchy, all the cantons of a tribe unite each year to organise a judicial circuit: the adult males from all the cantons assemble and assist the notables, who visit each village to pass sentence upon the year's criminals. (These notables often number about ten to a tribe; if the confederation is divided into four tribes it is clear why the notables are termed the *ait arba'in*.) The gathering of the whole tribe guarantees that the sentences are carried out.

Let us now leave the western High Atlas and turn to the Rif and the Jbala. Here again we find republics which have no moqaddem and which are frequently threatened by anarchy. Anarchy in the Rif has certain features that are so distinctive that we must describe them here and now. In the Rif, as elsewhere in the Berber regions, the smallest social group is the patriarchal family, while the larger groupings, here as elsewhere, are the canton and the tribe. But over much of this area internal conflicts and private feuds are so common that it is hardly possible to distinguish anything more than a confused mass of families fighting among themselves.

A village inhabited by the members of a single patriarchal family ends up, as a result of all these internal feuds, spread out along a hill ridge or across a flat hill-top. The fifty or so houses which comprise the village extend over perhaps two or three kilometres. Each house is built at some distance from its neighbour and is virtually a little fortress all on its own. The women leave the house in the morning before their husbands to make sure that no enemy is lurking in the vicinity; and the men keep their rifles beside them at all times, even when eating or praying. The dispersal of houses gives the countryside the appearance of 'stars in the sky', as the Riffians put it.

In the region inhabited by the Beni Wariaghel[3]—the compatriots of 'Abd el Krim—and among the tribes of the coastal areas, like the Boqqoia and Temsaman, who played an important part in the 1921-1926 rebellion, the only village will be that of a group of marabouts forming a collection of fifteen or so houses built close together. Everywhere else the houses are scattered in a way that reflects so well the anarchic nature of social organisation in the Rif. To illustrate the degree of violence that these private feuds can generate, we might give the example of two villages of the Ait 'Abdullah, of the Beni Wariaghel tribe. After the death of a dog belonging to a guest in one of the villages a conflict developed which lasted seven years and was responsible for fifty deaths on one side and seventy on the other. The defeated side fled to Zerhun after selling off their properties. With the cash realised by the sale of their land they hired killers to murder their enemies for a reward of fifty thousand francs.

Such relentlessness explains the long duration of these periods of hostilities in the Rif where each individual takes up arms to support

G

his neighbour. When a general weariness overtakes all the combatants the notables of the canton meet together and make a *ribat* in order to end the conflict. This is a solemn commitment to abstain from theft, murder, and so on, and to punish any harm done to women with great severity, for this is a common reason for an outbreak of hostilities. Huge fines, from ten thousand up to as much as fifty thousand francs, are exacted from those responsible for such acts. Peace reigns for perhaps a year or two and then, when someone infringes the law, a dispute will develop afresh over the sharing out of the fine.

It was from such a social background that 'Abd el Krim emerged, and the contrast between this anarchy and the law and order that he managed to impose gives a clear idea of the energy and authority required in order to build an embryo Riffian state. The republics of Kabylia before the French conquest were much more peaceful than those of the Rif, and they had reached, and even passed, the stage of stable government attained by the little states of the High Atlas with their councils and their moqaddems. Here, instead of the *inflas*, and *ait arba'in*, we find in each arsh a council of *temman* (authorities) assisted by *oqqal* (wise men); an amin presides over the council.

Here again, the republican form should not lead us to imagine that this is a democratic mode of government. Even when the whole mass of all the adult males is present at the meeting, it is only the elders who actually make the decisions. The deliberations of the legislative *jama'a* result finally in a proclamation of the decisions taken in council, rather than in a plebiscite. We know the amazing vitality of these oligarchic institutions in Kabylia. Today the arsh has ceased to be a political entity and activity centres on the village. There one still sees today the confrontation between the people and the council; the council of elders defending the traditions against the new demands made by the young men returning from factories in France, where they learned to liberate themselves from the narrow limits of tribal life. It was through observing the conflict between these two opposed tendencies that we learnt, twenty years ago, of the existence of illegal rulings in customary law (*qanun*) written in French which, without our knowledge, had for many years regulated social relations in the Kabyle villages. A fine example of the persistence of the Berber spirit in an area where, for sixty years, our administration has replaced the rule of the arsh.

We shall not develop the analysis of the political institutions of Berber cantons any further at this point. We should probably complete it with some discussion of the political organisation of the transhumants and nomads of the Central Atlas, the Sahara and the Aures, but in fact these supplementary data would add nothing substantially new to those which have served to provide the elements of a sketch of political organisation among the sedentary populations.

Before bringing this chapter to a close, however, it is necessary to draw attention to the fact that the political structure, although basically very uniform throughout the Berber areas, provides, nevertheless, certain minor variations from one canton to another. When one studies the social organisation of the small Berber republics of the High Atlas, for example, one is immediately struck by the fact that there is not one that has a political constitution exactly like that of its neighbours. There are always minor differences in the composition of the council, the changes of office, the mode of nomination of the moqaddem, and so on. There are, in short, differences in the structure of government among these little states in just the same way as there are differences between our great states in Europe. This variation is sufficient to show us how each of these political structures is a vital thing, and that it is, in every canton, not just a simple legacy from the past, but rather the result of unceasing activity on the part of the republic's leaders, or, if one prefers, the expression of the collective wisdom of the Berber social group.

Forms of Economic Cooperation

An analysis of the economic institutions also shows that the Berber communities do not limit themselves to the formulation of political constitutions and that, in this other sphere, the same ideal prevails; that is, to attempt a reconciliation between the love of anarchy and the benefits of cooperation. The sedentary Berber attempts, in all spheres of activity, to resolve the problems of daily life by some form of collective organisation, and for the most part he succeeds very well in this.

One of the primary opportunities for such forms of association is the corvée for agricultural purposes, or the *tuiza* as it is called. If an irrigation ditch needs repair, for instance, all the adult males are called together in a state of fasting (*hal saim*). The notables will take up their positions near the workers and drink tea at the expense of everyone else until the corvée has completed its task. The work will be finished quickly and the tribe—in the person of its leaders—will be honoured and rewarded. There are other types of tuiza: a corvée to collect dung, to assist a widow, to work for a marabout or to collect wood for the mosque. The general principle is to oblige all those who make use of it to provide their own services as well, either at the same time, or in turn, under threat of some penalty to be paid to the community at large or else to the leaders.

The love of cooperation—voluntary this time—is manifest in the way saline deposits are exploited. In the High Atlas there are saline springs where people come to draw water and then let it evaporate in small hollows dug out of the clay of a nearby hill. The segments of a family, once roughly equal at the time when the spring was first found or dug, find themselves of unequal status as a result of inheritance. They therefore constitute themselves freely into 'consumer associations', each having rights to the same number of buckets (two hundred, five hundred, eight hundred, or whatever) and each having its own day. In each group everyone will work together in a chain, pouring the water for each other into the hollows that they have excavated. Then they will gather to share out the precipitated salt among themselves.

Markets are also, in theory, communal institutions which the Berber republics attempt to regulate and to protect. They do not, however, always manage to do so. Certainly one finds the occasional large market protected by the council of notables and which provides important resources for the republic. In these cases they levy duties which go into the coffers of the canton treasury. But such cases are exceptional. Normally it is difficult for a Berber council to fulfil a policing role, maintaining order and controlling a market used by people from many different regions. It is possible at a pinch if the market is used only by the members of a single tribe, but if men from different tribes (who are often enemies) find themselves all mingling together, a council of notables which belongs to only a single canton has no hope of keeping the peace. Here one sees the essential weakness of the Berber republics. The difficulty may be solved by appealing to a single authority. Then, either the protection of a marabout is invoked, or else—and this is the more usual alternative —an *amghar*, or secular leader is used, for he is someone who speaks with enough authority for his word to be respected.

The same difficulties and the same solutions are to be found in the High Atlas, the Anti-Atlas, the Rif and Kabylia; and this has been so for a very long time. It is recorded that even as early as the Roman period there were markets in North Africa which belonged to important men, to rich and powerful leaders.[4] Berber society appears unchanging as regards its fundamental institutions.

Fortified Storehouses

It is in the founding and construction of the fortified storehouses, however, and in the development and running of these institutions, that the combined individualist and collectivist genius of the Berbers triumphs. As this institution is most highly developed in Morocco, and especially in the Anti-Atlas and the High Atlas, we shall describe the system prevailing in those areas. These fortified storehouses, which serve primarily as stores for family food (and particularly for grain) supplies, are found in many parts of North Africa. They have been reported from southern Tunisia, where they are called *ghorfa*, and among the transhumants of the Aures, under the name of *gela'a*. They are known as *igherm* or *tighermt* among the pastoralists of the Central Atlas, and as *agadir* in the settled parts of the Suss.

In this last region they have reached their highest point of perfection, to all appearances. They are vast storehouses built with several hundreds of little rooms and with three, four or five stories, on a plan which differs from canton to canton. Each family owns one or two rooms, either rooms originally built by one of their ancestors as a co-founder of the institution, or else rooms that have been bought at some time in the past. Thanks to the ramparts, the cistern and the watchtowers, the whole construction is a veritable fortress, within which the inhabitants of the canton or of the village can endure a long siege. Each family is often obliged to keep all its provisions, except those necessary for daily life, within the agadir.

These storehouse fortresses are organised according to customary legal rulings written in Arabic (for Berber is virtually never written) and dating back several centuries. They are compilations of two or three hundred clauses in proper books, preserved with religious care, which are designed to foresee all the problems that might arise regarding the respective rights and obligations of the users. They impose strict and heavy penalties upon sowers of discord and upon thieves, determine the collective responsibilities and set out the conditions under which the stores in the rooms may be used to provide collateral for loans or property transactions. These 'codes' would appear to be the most highly developed legal constructions that the Berbers have managed to produce by their own efforts. Some of them go back two or three centuries and the profusion of decrees and ordinances makes it possible to study their historical evolution and also the progressive transformation of Berber customary law.

If one tries to compare the different forms taken by these store-houses among the various Berber peoples of North Africa, one concludes that this institution may be seen as marking the transition from nomadic to settled life. Originally the pastoralist of the Sahara was content with a few hiding places in the rocks; then, when barley cultivation developed in the river valley bottoms, he dug a series of chambers in the cliffs, small caves in a regular pattern which were the first steps towards a storehouse proper. Next, caves began to be used, caves that were close to the group of tents and what soon became the first stone-built houses. This is the stage that has been reached today by the tribes of the Aures. Then the use of tents gradually declined and villages grew up around the fortified storehouses which, at the same time, became markets and centres for craftsmen. Finally, the spontaneous decline of the fortified storehouse is marked by the dispersal of artisans throughout the village and the subsequent birth of a town. We are dealing here, then, with an economic institution that has, from the very beginning, been very closely related to the life of the social group and been organised with the special care that reveals the Berber aptitude for cooperation.

The Modern Economy

The economic role of these fortified storehouses—which are survivals from the distant past and which, with the opening up of Berber society to world commerce, have rapidly disappeared—leads us to make a few remarks in conclusion about the changes that have taken place in Berber society as a result of contact with our industrial society.

The transformations brought about by our presence in North Africa are very considerable. These little cantons, which lived in virtual isolation, jealously sealed off from the outside world, where men lived by the grace of a primitive and feeble economy in a state of amazing self-sufficiency, found themselves thrust abruptly into contact with the modern world, and with an economy powerfully constituted to produce and consume.[5] The phenomenon of the dislocation of a primitive society resulting from this brutal contact has been described in many other countries by the term 'clash', and we shall not elaborate here on all the indications and consequences of this crushing process.

In Berber society one finds, as one finds elsewhere in the same circumstances, a decline in the primitive indigenous industries, a growth of exports of raw materials like wool, fruit, almonds and skins, and an associated increase in imports of manufactured goods and items like cotton, tea, coffee, rice and so on, demand for which grows rapidly greater, to the point where purchases soon exceed local resources. The cost of living has risen to thirty or forty times what it was previously over the past fifty years without any corresponding rise in purchasing power, and there is a marked tendency for extreme poverty to develop, for in such poor environmental conditions, where there is little specialisation or diversification, every crisis is deeply felt.

In such difficult circumstances it is interesting to see how fresh and energetic are the reactions of the settled Berber populations. All the able-bodied men demand from temporary migration the employment and resources denied them locally. Kabylia, the Rif and the Suss have, in this way, become reservoirs of labour for France and other parts of North Africa. One has observed the colonies of Shleuh and Kabyles grow up around Paris in such a regular fashion that one could produce a map of the Berber tribes of the Suss in the region around Paris. The Berbers come in fact to earn, with their labour, the cash necessary to keep alive the wives, children and old folk who have remained at home. In Morocco itself one sees the alternative route no less determinedly followed. The Shleuh settle in ever-growing numbers in the towns of the old Makhzen and, like the people of the Mzab in Algeria, begin as soon as they arrive to monopolise the small-scale commerce and even, as one can see happening in Rabat, Sala, Tangier and Fes, to displace the traditional urban bourgeoisie. Utilising family ties and kinship connections they establish companies, create subsidiaries one after the other—especially grocery businesses —and make their fortune in the city while at the same time running fleets of buses in order to maintain close ties with their region of origin. Others less able than these do, it is true, work in the factories and inhabit those cities of the poor, the *bidonvilles*, living gaily in their poverty.

These facts must be noted in addition to those relating to the political enterprises of local leaders—of which more shortly—because they underline, in a different way, the powerful vitality of the indigenous populations of Africa. Berber society reveals itself in advance to be capable of adapting itself, despite its primitive nature, if only we can see how to help and educate its members, to the most trying circumstances of modern life.

NOTES

1   This phrase of Montagne's, 'anarchie organisée', is identical to that used by Evans-Pritchard in his discussion of the political organisation of the Nuer, a tribal group of pastoralists living in the southern Sudan, in *African Political Systems*, edited by Fortes and Evans-Pritchard, p. 296. The similarity between the analysis of Nuer political structure by Evans-Pritchard and that of the Berbers by Montagne is extremely interesting and has been discussed by Gellner in his *Saints of the Atlas*. See also my Introduction for a brief comment.

2   The term 'notables' has considerable currency in both English and French literature on the Maghreb. As Waterbury notes, however, "the rural notables are, in part, a creation of the French administration of the bilad as-siba; it was, moreover, the French who insisted upon the word *notables* to designate this group". See Waterbury, *The Commander of the Faithful*, pp. 110-124.

3   A detailed account of the Ait Wariaghel of the central Rif will be found in David Hart's forthcoming book on the Ait Wariaghel. See also his article 'An Ethnographic Survey of the Riffian Tribe of Aith Waryaghil', in *Tamuda*, II, 1, 1954, pp. 51-86.

4   Discussion of the role and significance of tribal markets in Berber areas is to be found in the work of Benet, Fogg and Mikesell. See Bibliography.

5   There is good reason to believe that the popular image of a self-contained and insulated Morocco thrust suddenly into the modern world in the first decade of the twentieth century grossly underestimates the extent to which Morocco was involved in a wider economic and political system prior to the twentieth century. For some discussion of this question, see Miège's four-volume work *Le Maroc et l'Europe* and also Abun-Nasr's *A History of the Maghrib*. Chapters 1, 2 and 8 of *The Commander of the Faithful*, by Waterbury are also of interest in this connection.

IV

The Origins and Development of Power
among Temporal Leaders

Up until now we have been looking at the *static* aspect, if we might call it that, of Berber society; the structure of the small elementary states, the alliances which unite them one to another, the political and economic institutions patiently developed to reconcile the love of independence felt by every family with the benefits of cooperation in daily activities. We have thus sketched a picture of what one could call—using a somewhat pretentious term—'eternal Berber society'. This Berber society seems capable in fact of resisting all external assaults by virtue of its powerful traditions; it knows no other change than an infinitely gradual transformation, one perhaps a hundred or a thousand times as slow as that undergone by our own Western states. The consequences of this process of change appear only in the formation of slightly more concentrated states, in the establishment of more densely congregated villages, and in the gradual disappearance of the communal fortresses. This alteration is so slow that the Berber societies we can observe directly give us the impression of remaining absolutely stationary, and we are able to perceive the changes only by comparing different groups in North Africa with one another.

It remains for us now to describe what we might call the *dynamic* aspect of Berber society.[1]

The grip of the republican and anarchic tradition is not so strong that there do not constantly emerge in North Africa, within several of the five or six thousand little elementary states which cover the mountain regions of the Maghreb, ambitious and energetic men capable of setting themselves above the councils of notables. These leaders establish states of varying sizes, by violence or by political manœuvring; and there are even those who manage to build chiefdoms, kingdoms and empires. The great speed with which these men achieve their task of unifying and centralising the political system is in direct contradiction with the conservative force of Berber tradition. We observe also that the decline of the states that they found is often as swift as their emergence was sudden. The existence of these political leaders reveals the presence in the Maghreb of forces both for construction and destruction, long repressed by tradition.

First of all we shall describe the initial stages in the rise to power of such leaders, how they take over a canton, then a tribe, and then one or more confederations, to become what we have called in the Atlas 'the great qāids'. We shall see finally how the action of the Arab Makhzen completes their work by completely destroying the traditional, anarchic Berber society and replacing that complex patchwork of little states with a single, unified and absolute state, within which men are blindly subjected to a single master, as may be seen in the kingdoms of the east. At the same time we shall discuss how social organisation in the Makhzen areas differs from that which was occasionally achieved in the past by Berber empire builders.

In order to set out the successive stages in the rise to power of political leaders, we shall retain the method used so far—a method rendered valid by the cellular structure of Berber society—the comparative method. Berber leaders emerge in all regions, but some of them, at certain periods, provide us with more numerous examples than do the others. It will be sufficient if we choose the most characteristic, then by comparing them with each other we shall be able to see easily what laws determine the behaviour of such leaders and control the stages of their political manœuvring, probably without their being aware of it.

The Emergence of the Amghar

How is it possible for a leader to take over a canton which has, up until that time, been governed as a Berber republic? Let us look at the Moroccan High Atlas, where we have already described the organisation of the oligarchic republics with their senate (the *inflas* or *ait arba'in*) and their president elected for a year or chosen by casting lots (the moqaddem). This region has, in fact, over three generations between 1890 and 1925 seen the rise of some fifty or so small leaders or 'amghars', as they are called in these parts. Of these only six or seven managed to extend their influence and authority beyond the canton and take over a tribe, while three became great qāids, lords of small princedoms.

The egalitarianism which exists within a council of notables in a Berber republic is purely nominal. Despite the respect paid to egalitarian institutions, even in those regions where public opinion is most critical—to such an extent that the rich have houses that are no finer than those of the poor—one finds that it is the rich who exercise power behind the scenes. There are generally three or four notables in the council of *inflas* who secretly compete for power and for the council's funds. When an ambitious man sets himself to manipulate the constitution nothing can prevent him from corrupting the other members of the council. In such cases one finds him remaining in office as moqaddem for several years, in contravention of custom which demands that this responsibility be limited to periods of one year only, and inviting the council frequently to his own home to treat its members with great generosity; also he provides huge meals for his friends and dresses with considerable elegance. The share of the fines paid by those guilty of crimes that he awards himself becomes ever greater, while that allocated to the masses and to the notables without influence becomes smaller and smaller. One day he gives himself the title of *amghar** (political leader) and as long as he is strong enough to maintain his position no one dares any longer to ask him to submit to election procedures in the same way as they would a simple moqaddem.

The new leader does not always have an easy start. Within the canton, in fact, it is rare that there is no opposing faction led by another man of ambition whose influence may equal that of our new amghar. Most frequently, conflict breaks out within the little state, and it is the more powerful of the two who emerges victorious, the other being killed or exiled together with all his supporters. Doomed is the amghar who launches forth upon the hazardous career of a political leader without having first established unity within the canton, by underhand means if necessary. The man who fails to establish the control of all other rival families by his own as the first step of all will find himself abandoned at the first crisis. One could give numerous examples of such cases, but let us just take that of a

---

* From the Berber root M Gh R—to be old or great by virtue of age or status. The term corresponds to the Arabic *shaykh*. In the Central Atlas it is sometimes used in a different sense when the amghar may be elected (*amghar n-tuga*), but, in order to avoid confusion, we shall use the term amghar only to refer to the political leader who has seized power by force and who is a tyrant in the true, historical sense of the word.

small amghar of the Seksawa, Si Mokhtar, son of Hammo u Bella who, over twenty-five years, made himself master of a tribe by his own efforts alone and who died nineteen years ago, before the subjection of his people by the French.

Around 1860 his father was moqaddem of a canton and had kept power without wishing to eliminate the heads of neighbouring families, who were extremely envious of his position. He left to wage war against an adjoining canton but his followers deserted him when it came to the fighting and he was obliged to give up all claims to leadership and go into exile, thus losing all his possessions. When the son, Si Mokhtar, was, in his turn, through favourable circumstances, able to seize power in 1880, he invited all his enemies and rivals to a magnificent feast to celebrate the reconciliation of all the previously warring factions. Then, apparently determined that evening to unite the tribe completely, he organised dances in the village square in the light thrown out by great bonfires. When the sound of singing filled the valley he offered tea to his four rivals—now his friends—and very quietly, in a small room, had their throats cut by his brothers. For him this was the first step in a career full of political and military success, that was to last for forty years.

What inhibits the first efforts of the would-be amghar the most is the poverty of his financial resources. The Berber mountains are poor and a flock of a thousand sheep and a few terraced fields along a river bank will not be enough to finance major political enterprises. Certainly there are the fines paid by offenders, but the rates cannot be too exorbitant or they run the risk of provoking rebellion. The adult males of a canton would generally also accept an annual tax of one or two measures of barley and the third required by the '*ashur*—the Qur'anic tax which, until this stage, is given entirely to marabouts or to the poor. But their willingness to contribute in this fashion is limited to these forms of levy in most cases. It then becomes necessary to look elsewhere.

The amghar seeks to utilise his primary resources in order to cut a chiefly figure within the group, and to invite the notables of neighbouring cantons to his house in order to create for himself the reputation of a generous man. As soon as possible after this stage he tries to become the leader of his leff. We have already described these alliances between cantons, these sorts of territorial bloc by means of which a small state finds help against a hostile neighbour, by having him opposed on the other side by another canton in such a way that the whole region comes to resemble a chequer-board of two opposing colours, whose 'squares' are the hostile cantons fixed in enmity towards one another for generations. It is upon this chequer-board that the ambitious would-be amghar plays his political game. He tries, with all the means at his disposal, to stir up hatred between the two leffs, he intervenes in all quarrels and brings the support of his own fighting men to the assistance of all his leff brothers, even if they live a long way away. All the people of the canton involved in this external conflict help themselves at the expense of the traditional enemy, pillage his fields, burn his houses and drive off his animals. Through its involvement in such activities the little state of the aspiring amghar retains its solidarity and internal discord is reduced or else forgotten. At the same time, the leader enriches himself, his reputation grows, his house is enlarged and he continues to climb the rungs of power little by little.

His rule has not, as yet, altered the external forms of the former type of anarchic government. The *inflas* still exist, but they meet now at his house and make sure that they take no decisions with which he would not agree. Custom continues to be respected, so long as it does not go against the interests of the leader. There are no new taxes. In short, the rule of the amghar at the beginning is easy enough for his fellow canton members. It is only the neighbouring cantons, those of the opposing leff, who have anything to complain about. It remains for them, in order to protect themselves, to rally around a leader in the same way as their enemies have done; in this fashion the rival leader consolidates the forces of his alliance. Thus the torch of war is lit and it burns for many years across the territories of whole tribes at a time, while they exhaust themselves in their efforts to range an equal number of dead on either side, so as to be able one day to conclude an honourable peace agreement.

The general conditions under which an amghar emerges in the independent mountain republics are very similar in all the Berber areas: in the Anti-Atlas, in the Rif and in Kabylia. The only difference is that in the Anti-Atlas and the Rif the chequer-board of leffs is composed of larger 'squares'—of tribes and confederations— which are too great for the leader of a canton to be able to play an important role as easily. In these parts, moreover, the amghar strengthens his position by making use of disputes and cleavages that are more recent than those of the leffs, but he soon manages by his personal manœuvres to create two blocs of alliances very like those that we have described for the High Atlas.

In the Anti-Atlas public opinion is more strongly opposed to the emergence of an amghar, while in the Rif the widespread existence of anarchy and interpersonal conflict is hardly favourable for the concentration of political power. In Kabylia, for the same reason, the existence of soffs, which divide the region, not into two blocs of cantons, but into two blocs comprising villages or parts of villages, constitutes an obstacle to the unification of the canton (or arsh) under the control of a single leader. The Rif and Kabylia thus offer a better field of action for the marabouts (the religious leaders) who also know the secret of utilising and living off the cleavages that exist within Berber society, but in their case by knowing how to reduce and to mediate these cleavages.

The Consolidation of Power

The Berber amghar has not really raised himself above the confines of the anarchic republic until he has succeeded in breaking out of the strict limits of the canton and in dominating a whole tribe. If he manages to crush the opposing leff in the neighbourhood of his own supporting cantons, to assassinate the amghar of the other faction or to seize his lands, he has taken yet another step (and a decisive one this time) towards undisputed power. In order to do this he requires certain favourable conditions, which occur only occasionally. But the downfall of the main rival is soon exploited; the men of the leff of the victorious amghar invade the villages of the defeated one and raze them to the ground, while the local inhabitants flee into exile, taking with them whatever they can save of their flocks. The successful amghar cultivates the fields of his rival, stores up the harvested crops and soon builds there a fortress in which he establishes his brother together with a loyal garrison selected from the new leader's own canton. From this point onwards he begins to consolidate his state. The boundaries are roughly those of a tribe comprising the cantons of the two leffs. In his own leff the amghar continues to respect the republican institutions of the other cantons provided his own overall authority is not questioned; in the leff of the defeated rival he will nominate lesser amghars or *shaykhs* who will be his minions and who will be responsible for collecting taxes on his behalf.

In this way one may observe the changes that take place in the canton from which the amghar originally came, particularly with regard to the external forms of government. The amghar generally has himself built a qasbah, apart from his kinsmen's village; this building is already a fortress and it seems to have been constructed as much to resist the enemy from outside as to control his own village. Above all, it has an important annexe; a thing unknown until this point in any Berber area: a prison. Customary law does not envisage imprisonment under any circumstances; all penalties are paid on the spot: fine, exile or sometimes mutilation, sometimes even death. Now the amghar, setting himself above the traditions of the assembly, puts his enemies out of harm's way, and also, sometimes, his friends if they forget to obey his orders. And, while one knows very well when one enters the dungeon of the amghar, one can never tell when one will leave. Generally prisoners die there as a result of the miserable conditions, unless poison is introduced into their food to put an end to their suffering.

The amghar gathers around him a guard composed of slaves and mercenaries; his kinsmen assist him in governing and controlling the subject cantons. Little by little leff conflict dies away all around; it is no longer the time for fighting, the fields must be cultivated and the gardens irrigated in order to scrape together enough for the tribute exacted by the lord of the qasbah.

In the High Atlas there have been six or seven amghars of this kind since 1850: Mohammed des Ind Maghus, amghar of the mountain Gedmiua; Si Mokhtar of the Seksawa; the father of Si Taieb Gontafi (between 1860 and 1880); Mohammed, the father of the Glawi (at the outset); Mohammed Ibibat, and Bu Naga of the Ida u Tanan. It would not be quite correct to say that these leaders appeared automatically in the vicinity of the mountain passes; the origins of their authority have nothing to do with tolls exacted from travellers. One can only observe that those who rose to power in the neighbourhood of the major mountain routes entered into relations with the Makhzen with greater facility, received its support—often after having originally resisted it, as in the case of Gontafi—and ended up by acquiring three times the power by subduing vast areas in the name of the Sultan. But it would be greatly over-simplifying the situation to explain the emergence of these major leaders in terms of a simple topographical determinism. The primary factors affecting a leader's rise to power are social, and it is the Berber political game which determines the phases in the emergence of the amghar.

Let us repeat, once more, that the temporal Berber leader has no magical powers. We know that among many primitive communities, and especially in Black Africa, the growing power of the chief is associated with a host of religious or magical attributes; to such an extent that he frequently appears as a sort of priest-king. Certainly one finds traces of magical powers in Berber society; we have already mentioned above the 'luck-bearing' *inflas*, who bear the same title as the political *inflas* (the notables of the canton council). There are also agricultural 'kings' who appear, as in many other countries, at harvest time, but these have no importance in political life and their 'reign' lasts only for a few hours in a field full of sheaves of corn.

In fact the Berber amghar must not be confused with the king or chief in other primitive societies. The social relations that he has with the tribe and the mechanics of his rise, place him rather with the 'tyrant' of Greek society in the eighth century BC, before the cities had developed their political institutions. The king, clothed in magical and religious power, is represented in Berber society by the marabout. Solidarity is created in this case not by violence, but by respect for him because his power is beneficent for men, animals and harvests, and because his curse is feared. The amghar, for his part, is nothing but a despotic leader, whom one helps for a while, whom one supports, but who disappears one day together with the state he founded because his sons are no longer sufficiently energetic to keep a hold of the thousand political intrigues of tribal politics.

The 'Great Qāid'

It now remains for us to give some idea of the authority of those most powerful of all Berber leaders, who are no longer found today except in the region to the south of Marrakesh, and who have been hailed in the literature as 'The Lords of the Atlas'.[2] (This literature has, unfortunately, frequently misrepresented our policy towards the tribes and has cost the common people dear. But these 'romancers' are irresponsible.)

It is not true that we are dealing here with an ancient form of power, for this would be in contradiction with all that we know, up until now, of the anarchic nature of Berber society. It is not true that these mountain lords have controlled the tribes who live under their authority today for generations past, as they themselves often allow over-credulous travellers to believe. On the contrary, the establishment of the great qāids of the Atlas is a very recent phenomenon. They took control of their present domains in the years of general chaos and upheaval—of *siba*[3]—that followed the death of Sultan Moulay el Hassan between 1894 and 1902.

Until that time, in fact, the three leaders who were to become the great qāids of the Atlas—el Mtuggi, qāid of the little tribe of the Mtugga; el Gontafi, independent amghar from Tagontaft who became qāid of the tribe of l-Asif Nefis; and el Glawi, qāid of the

little tribe of the Glawa—were mere officials of the central government, very like the other petty despots of the mountain regions. The
first belonged to a family devoted to the Makhzen for over a century,
the second had succeeded in seizing, by his own efforts, the territory
that the Sultan later conceded to him in order to make use of this
Berber amghar's ambitions to further his own Sherifian plans and
policies, the third, a qāid and son of a small shaykh and leader of a
canton, was charged from time to time with the task of collecting
taxes on the Sultan's behalf in the regions to the south of the
Atlas.

In each of these three domains it happened that ambitious young
men took power after the deaths of their fathers between 1880 and
1888; but during the reign of the energetic Moulay el Hassan none of
them dared extend the limits of his territory and wage war upon his
neighbours. The petty 'chief' of the Glawa, Si el Madani, received in
1891 as a gift from the Sultan a small cannon which the Sultan gave
him during his journey to Taluet on his return from an expedition in
Tafilalet. It was at about this time that modern weapons (rifles with
cartridges, etc.) were making their appearance in Morocco.⁴ El
Mtuggi and el Gontafi both built up supplies of these arms, buying
them on the black market from the Christians and Jews of Mogador.
Finally, on the death of the Sultan, the aggressive ambitions of the
three Berber amghars, so long repressed, could at last be freely
expressed. Taking advantage of the state of siba between 1894 and
1897 they conquered the neighbouring tribes with the help of their
own loyal supporters. Then, soon afterwards, they headed towards
the richer lands of the Suss valley and the foothills on the side of the
mountains facing Marrakesh. Very soon they began to fall out among
themselves, and for two years they devoted themselves to a bitter
internecine struggle. It was Gontafi, on the whole, who suffered most
from the simultaneous assaults of his two rivals, situated as he was in
between them.

The fortunes of the Glawa began to improve, especially when Si el
Madani, who had supported the pretender Moulay Hafid, managed
to get himself appointed Grand Vizir to his protégé, who became
Sultan in Fes. They then became rulers over numerous tribes at the
wishes of the Makhzen. The downfall of Moulay Hafid put a halt to
their expansion. It was then that the south of Morocco shook with
the storm raised by the son of Ma el 'Ainin, el Hiba—sultan of the
holy war and Mehdi, who came from the desert of Mauritania. He
proclaimed the rule of justice and gave the signal to the masses,
oppressed by the great amghars, for a new period of siba. The great

H

qāids felt the security of their positions threatened and, as soon as the French victory at Sidi bu Otman was confirmed, they declared their loyalty to the new Makhzen.

For fifteen years they were to hold their mountain domains without change, trying to conceal from our eyes (as did the Mtugga) the existence of dissident groups of the high valleys like the Seksawa and the Gedmiua, who rebelled against their authority and remained more or less faithful to their oligarchic councils or to their little amghars. They continued to assure their position of domination by cleverly placing themselves at our service (as did the Glawa leaders) and by taking considerable material advantage of the situation at the same time and crushing their new subjects with taxes to such an extent that they used up the region's resources for a generation. The deaths of Mtuggi and of Gontafi ensured a change of regime in the administration of their territories and, little by little, at the same time, the vast domain of the Glawa opened up to fall under our authority.

What characterised the administration of the Lords of the Atlas above all was the preponderant role played by those loyal elements who supported their programme of conquest from the very beginning. The cantons from which they themselves came originally provided the great lords with tax collectors, 'khalifas' and shaykhs, and it was from the families of their own villages especially that they selected the greatest number of officials. Their initial leff, and even all of their tribe, provided garrison troops in abundance for the occupation of qasbahs in distant provinces, or for a reliable guard to accompany them on expeditions of conquest. This military organisation was complemented by an important institution at home—the placing of hired men, and more particularly of slaves, in charge of the administration of their domains, now enlarged out of all proportion by confiscation or purchase.

As the power of the amghar grew, so did his qasbah and those of his kinsmen which were built in the vicinity. The centre of his domain became a veritable small town in the heart of the mountains. In their enlarged fortresses they enjoyed a life that was more comfortable than that of the qāids of the Makhzen. They constantly increased the number of their slaves and of their wives; they exchanged their daughters among themselves and were continually contracting new marriages for political reasons. The normal pattern of the Berber family—which was strictly monogamous—was abandoned, and they were imitated by all their officials and close kinsmen at their 'court'.

Finally, in the tribes themselves the earlier institutions dating from the period of independence and the mountain republics became more and more eroded. The wishes of the great lord replaced the law and there was no longer room for the councils of notables in his qasbah. Little by little also the quarrels between leffs were forgotten as acquaintance with the chequer-board of hostile and friendly cantons became less, being replaced by the loyalty of a group of supporters to their great lord, except, perhaps, in the high valley regions whose remoteness and poverty protected them from the expansionist policies of the Masters of the Qasbahs.

This new form of government dominating the region, however, was able to maintain itself only by exacting ever heavier taxes from the subject tribes. From this point onwards the Berbers were obliged to direct all their efforts towards their fields and their flocks. Despite all their exertions they had little with which to produce the amounts required by the great lord, and often in fact the heavy burden imposed upon them brought about the speedy impoverishment of the region. The independent mountain communities had passed away, and from this point onwards the Berbers were prepared to endure the yoke of the Makhzen, which came in its turn to replace the Lords of the Atlas and to mark the final stage in the political transformation of Berber society.

The Fragility of the Amghar's Power

In order to complete this analysis of the forms that the authority of the political leader takes in Berber society, let us set out clearly in conclusion the simple mechanism by which his emergence and rise to power takes place. In a canton the aspiring amghar gains control thanks to the support of a loyal faction based on his own patriarchal family and upon those whom he rallies to his side to combat the opposition that inevitably develops within the anarchic republic. In a tribe he triumphs because of the strength of his leff which is able to defeat the opposing leff; and, in short, he exploits the tribe with the support of the fighting men of his own canton, assisted by those of his own leff. In a larger field still, the great qāid subdues tribes and confederations with troops provided by his own tribe. He gives the remunerative task of collecting taxes from remote districts to fellow members of his canton and tribe. It is essentially the exploitation of a whole area by a single tribe.

This concentric structure of the Berber state founded by force explains the facility with which it is established and organised, but it also explains, at the same time, the speed of its disintegration. The central core is easily dislocated. In a canton or tribe the family of the great leader may not be perfectly united, and, even more significantly, the son or grandson does not always have the qualities of the original founder of the state. They have not grown up in the midst of conflict and their hand has not the same cunning. Revolts are quick to break out, and when they do take place the cantons revive their former councils of notables without difficulty and return to the ideal of ordered anarchy well known to their ancestors almost as soon as they are released from the grip of their overlord. Customary law flourishes again, the tribal fortresses are relieved and people begin again to quarrel among themselves—a pleasure that they had not experienced in a long while.

In the families which control these huge domains, where the traditional monogamous pattern of the Berber family is most drastically altered, the presence of children belonging to women of different backgrounds (slaves, peasant women and daughters of the urban bourgeoisie) is a permanent source of strife. The government itself becomes feeble and, at the same time, the lethargy of the tribes, exhausted by years of exploitation, reaches its maximum. The smallest outbreak of siba, the least dynastic dispute in the Bled el Makhzen, threatens to light a blaze which will quickly spread through the mountain areas. The qasbahs close their doors, the tribes besiege them, and a long period of anarchy is enough to cause all that imposing 'feudal' façade to crumble into dust. It was, as we have said, the fear that such a catastrophe w_: imminent that pushed the great qāids of the Atlas to rally to the support of the French in 1912, after the great xenophobic and popular uprising that el Hiba led against Marrakesh.

No 'Berber Feudalism'

The term 'feudal' has sometimes been used to refer to this form of political system created by Berber leaders in the Atlas, especially when referring to the tribal amghars or to the great qāids. Was there really a Berber feudal system? First of all, we do not find in Morocco that hierarchic power structure which characterises European feudalism. The Berber leader is by no means always subject to the control of the Sultan; and when he is, the ties that hold him are fragile and can be broken without any formal procedure if one or other of the parties has the strength to break them. Nor is there any equivalent of the feudal courts, where a baron could be accused before his peers. Most important of all, there is nothing like the bonds which tied subjects to the land; no 'leaseholds' or 'freeholds', as in our Middle

Ages. Private ownership, which is most widely found in Berber areas, exists everywhere. The property of the qāid certainly sometimes includes, as a result of seizure or of purchase, the property of his subjects, who then become mere farmers; but as soon as he is deposed the former owners of the land recover their property and life continues as before. Finally, the precarious nature of this system of domination should rule out the use of the term 'feudal' which in the West at least refers to a very stable form of political organisation. That our feudal system could last, despite its faults and even its iniquities, for ten centuries until the Revolution is at least an indication that an acceptable equilibrium had been established between rulers and ruled, and that, over the centuries, the advantages gained by the feudal lords through their position of dominance were balanced by the services they performed. Had this not been so the serfs would have swept it away much sooner. In Berber society the tribal rebellion is rarely long delayed and the absolute power of the rulers never lasts for more than two or three generations.

In fact the only term which really could be applied to this form of organisation is that which Foucauld used a long time ago: 'the despotic regime'. It drains the life from a region and is not able, because of its own fragility, to establish lasting institutions.[5]

Given such a political system, one is tempted in one's heart of hearts to take the side of the Berber republics. It seems as though all the goodness and right is on their side. Why then are we so deeply associated with the qāids? Is this proof of a machiavellian conspiracy on the part of the Makhzen or of the French authorities? In fact the rationale behind this collaboration between the qāids and the central government is quite simple. It is that it is practically impossible to deal with a Berber republic, when one adopts the point of view that takes the general good into consideration. It requires years of patience to get a council to take decisions about such things as the reorganisation of the region, the building of roads, the payment of taxes and the exercise of justice. All the time one would be held up by continual discussion and countless insignificant complaints. There is no place for the ordered anarchy of the Berber cantons in a modern state.

There is no other way to control and reorganise Berber society than to deal first of all with the leaders, controlling their activities and reprimanding their excesses, which is certainly not always easy. Then one will witness the growth of what is the greatest problem of all in the administration of Berber areas; the fact that, in the eyes of the population, and of the chiefs, during the period before our arrival, law and order was synonymous with boundless tyranny and ruin for the majority, while anarchy appeared, as did general lack of law and order, as a form of justice and a precondition for individual prosperity. The modification of such ideas in the minds of the people and their leaders and the implementation of a form of administration that is at the same time just, orderly and profitable, is not the least of the difficult tasks now facing France.

NOTES

1 The distinction made here by Montagne between the *static* and *dynamic* aspects of Berber society is crucial to his analysis and it sets him apart from his British contemporaries, whose analyses were almost entirely static. The distinction was not, however, unknown to British anthropologists. See Radcliffe-Brown's *Structure and Function in Primitive Societies*, and Firth's *Essays on Social Organisation and Values*.

2 E.g. Gavin Maxwell's *Lords of the Atlas: the Rise and Fall of the House of Glaoua, 1893-1956*.

3 Siba has been translated as 'dissidence', 'disorder', 'anarchy' and 'insolence'. The nature of the relationship between *'bled el makhzen'* and *'bled es siba'* is itself controversial and the precise translation of the word *'siba'* depends to a large extent upon the view one holds of the structure and organisation of the pre-colonial state in Morocco. Some reference to this difficult, but crucial, topic is made in my Introduction, but see also Lahbabi, *Le Gouvernement Marocain à l'Aube du XXe Siècle*; Gellner's comments on the problem in *Saints of the Atlas*; and Waterbury's characterisation in Chapters 1 and 3 of *The Commander of the Faithful*. I have left the word untranslated in order to allow the multiple interpretation of the concept.

4 The rapid spread of repeating rifles in the late nineteenth century had a substantial effect on tribal politics and on the balance of power between *makhzen* and *siba*. Gun-running into Morocco had been a profitable enterprise for European dealers since the middle of the fifteenth century.

5 Probably the most complete analysis of European feudalism is to be found in Marc Bloch's *Feudal Society*. See also the stimulating discussion by Godelier in 'La notion de "mode de production asiatique" et les schémas marxistes d'évolution des sociétés' in C.E.R.M., *Sur le Mode de Production Asiatique*.

V

The Transformation of Berber Society

It now remains for us to describe the final stage in the transformation of the society: the establishment of kingdoms and empires built out of the ruins of Berber republics.

These great states belong to two different categories. Either they are Arab empires—like those, for instance, of the Sa'dian and Filalian *shorfa*—which existed for four centuries in Morocco and which absorbed the Berber tribes little by little, or else they are Berber empires, born in the mountains, which build up a number of subject territories around a central core and which gradually expand into the plains, tending to lose in the final stages of their short existence any memory of their origins and to evolve in much the same way as the states in the first category from that point onwards.[1]

The Sultan's Government

Let us examine the elements from which these empires are constructed. What is—or rather, what was before the establishment of the Protectorate—the social organisation of the Berber tribes, whether Arabised or not, in the Bled el Makhzen? What constitutes the Makhzen in the eyes of the tribes is a Sultan of Sherifian origin, whether real or fictional, and an army which maintains law and order and also collects taxes. The Sultan (*l-agellid*, as they call him among the Berber tribes) is a person to be respected and feared, even when one is not ruled by him. He is, even for the independent tribes of the mountains, a man above all others and of a different kind. We see here a recurrence of the anthropolatrous tendencies of the Berbers; the tendency that is fully satisfied when they live under the political

control of a marabout. The Sultan has supernatural powers, at least
this was believed to be so twenty years ago; during the reign of a
good Sultan everyone knows that the harvests are rich and the flocks
prosper and flourish. His curse (*sokhta*) is greatly feared by the tribes
as the people of the Middle Ages might have feared excommunica-
tion. The sokhta, applied to a dissident tribe, authorises first of all the
general pillage of the property of those cursed; but what is still more
terrible is that it renders the earth barren and produces famine. The
example of what befell the tribe of the Haha in 1847, threatened by
the Sultan with divine vengeance after the sack of Mogador, still
remains in the memories of the inhabitants of southern Morocco.
This dangerous power of the Sultan's is an attribute consequent upon
his descent from the Prophet; furthermore, all the rulers since the
time of the Almohads have contrived to fabricate 'sherifian' genealo-
gies, even when they were pure Berbers. This tradition is so well
preserved that even today one finds the great Berber qāids construct-
ing noble Arab family trees for themselves and, in their later years,
even becoming '*sherifs*'.

The Sultan is, therefore, respected as a sherif, even when his
secular authority is rejected. His person may not be harmed even
when his armies are defeated. When the Berbers of the Middle Atlas
stripped or killed all the followers of the Sultan Moulay Sliman at the
beginning of the nineteenth century they treated the sovereign himself with due respect and escorted him back to the safety of the plains.

We shall not describe here the antiquated and picturesque court of
the Sultan of Morocco. This has been done very often and we refer
the reader, for such a description, to Erckmann's book, *Modern
Morocco*, written during the reign of Moulay el Hassan by this
perceptive eye-witness.

The administration of the Sultan is primitive and rudimentary. It
consists of a 'vizir' or minister (one only), a *hajib* (a sort of master of
the palace), various secretaries with poorly defined tasks, the
company of *msakhrin* (or messengers) charged with carrying out
expeditionary missions, and the gīsh, or troops recruited from among
the Arabised tribes settled around the towns. This, at least, is how the
Makhzen used to be. We should look a little more closely, however,
at one of the crucial forces at the disposal of the Sherifian government: the army.

The Sherifian army comprises three elements: the gīsh, who
occasionally revolt and force the Sultan to transfer their tribes from

one capital to another; black slaves who, in the eighteenth century, were the architects of bloody uprisings and rebellions without number throughout the country; and troops recruited on the spot from among the Arab or Berber tribes as the *mehalla* of the Makhzen passes through their territory. The primary function of the Sherifian army is to undertake tax-collecting expeditions. We know how difficult it has always been to maintain the organisation of a Muslim state on the bases laid down by the Holy Book without adding the *kharaj* (a tax imposed upon infidels) to the *zekkat* (the Qur'anic tax of the faithful). In a country where all the subjects are Muslims and where the kharaj has no application it is necessary to raise taxes at all costs, even if it has to be done illegally. The Sultan's army (*harka*) takes care of this and gathers contributions from the tribes whose total easily exceeds the amount defined as religious tax. In practice the amount that each tribe contributes depends on the strength of the Sherifian mehalla or upon how close it passes to the region. When the Makhzen forces actually enter one's territory one is at their mercy and crushing amounts may be paid as tax; at the same time there is a very real risk that one's grain silos will be emptied as further pay-ment. If they remain a fair distance away it is enough to send them a few mules as tribute. Often hostages are taken to ensure payment.

As soon as the army leaves the region the Berber tribes often drive away into exile the qāids who have been set up over them. But if the Makhzen is strong in that region the qāids installed by the mehalla have a more lasting authority. They maintain law and order in the tribe, collect taxes and execute the judgements of the *qadi* (the religious judge who replaces the council of notables in such areas). It is important to note that the qāid directly under the control of the Makhzen, whose position can be destroyed at the mere whim of the Sultan, rarely has the support of more than a small group of loyal tribesmen from one privileged canton. On the other hand, he recruits his supporters in a more haphazard fashion from various parts of his domain and reinforces them with slaves. The abuses to which he subjects the tribes: corvées, expropriation of lands and the imposition of unofficial taxes, enable him to grow rich quickly. But if he dies or is deposed it is the Makhzen that inherits all those possessions acquired by him during his period of office. This simple method whereby the expropriated goods 'revert to the treasury' was, in the old Makhzen, a natural corollary of, and corrective to, the corruption of officials. Some regret the passing of this tradition.

Some Sultans—Moulay el Hassan for example—appointed special officials (*umana*) to be responsible for guarding the property of the

Makhzen and for controlling the excesses of the qāids. But such attempts have no real effect; qāids and *umana* soon manage to come to some agreement about how to milk the people in their charge. The Makhzen often shows evidence of considerable skill in the way in which it managed the administration of the Berber areas. At the outset it often nominates a shaykh or qāid for each canton, then, taking advantage of favourable circumstance, it generally eliminates the smaller officials and replaces them with a single overall administrator who can control the whole region (that is, one or more tribes), with less expenditure and, at the same time, exact the maximum of taxes. If this official becomes too powerful his province is broken up after his dismissal or death (this last being occasionally carefully arranged) and given to a rival family. Soon the development of the influence of the Makhzen generates a new set of social groupings. We have already spelled out the vital significance of the canton (that basic political cell of Berber society) under the oligarchic regime. The canton has endured, from the early days of subjection to the Makhzen and throughout the period of control by a great Berber qāid of the mountains. Later on it is no longer controlled by a council of notables or even by an amghar; or, at least, the amghar has come to be called by the Arabic name of shaykh. When the tribe is fully absorbed into the Makhzen an important change takes place. The Sherifian government replaces the traditional division into cantons by a new form of division, completely arbitrary this time, which divides the region into units of taxation. Under this system the tribe is divided into ten *mia* (ten 'hundreds' of households, in principle); or, alternatively, into five, six or eight *khums*, where before it had been composed of four or five cantons. Sometimes a khums is half a canton in the north and an isolated village in the south. Often it is a shaykh who collects the taxes (we can hardly say who administers) in this new unit which includes such disparate elements.

This new Makhzen-style subdivision of the countryside, whose existence may be observed all along the edges of the recently absorbed Berber areas (although there may remain a few remnants here and there of the earlier form of organisation) has considerable importance. It manages to obliterate all memories, both of local conflicts (the basis of which was the leff) and, even more particularly, of the councils of notables, which were always ready to reconstitute themselves in times of revolt or of siba. The Berber way of life, eliminated at the level of the canton, finds refuge in the village, the hamlet and the household.

Tribal law (*'urf*) suffers considerably in the reorganisation of the region. It could be said that the Makhzen only tolerates these bodies of customary law (some of which, like those which relate to the collective storehouses, to the use of irrigation ditches, to access to grazing grounds, and to the protection of the harvest, have a considerable influence on the organisation of social groups), where it is able to suppress them entirely. Certainly particularly wise and politically adept Sultans have granted the Berber populations of areas like the Suss the right to continue to make use of these publicly useful laws, as did Moulay el Hassan between 1880 and 1886 during his expedition to the Suss.

But, for the most part, the local official of the Makhzen (the qāid) regards such a body of law as a dangerous reminder of the time when the tribe was composed of autonomous republics. And his subjects feel the same way.

It is generally felt, in most regions, that when the Sultan is in control of the area law and order is maintained but justice is not always upheld. When the tribe revolts, on the other hand, and when anarchy and disorder are at their height, customary law is revived once more, as far as is possible, in order to provide each with his due and to punish each according to his crime. In practice, under the Makhzen, the books of customary law are placed in the hands of the shaykh or qāid, who make use of it only when they find articles that support their own judgement. The rest of the time, they make judgements according to their own lights, or else have the problem settled by the qadi, who, as everyone is aware, may be an independent judge in theory, but is, in practice, humbly devoted to serving the Makhzen official and obliges him who offers the most. As for the tribal fortresses, if they have somehow managed to survive the rule of the amghar, they are destroyed on the orders of the Makhzen. The most striking consequences of this regime of oppression are, first of all, the economic impoverishment of the region, which in the eyes of the Makhzen official has certain advantages in so far as it weakens the men of the tribe, prevents them from rising in revolt and keeps them quiet; and secondly, the development of siba, or revolt, some time later. In areas under nominal Makhzen control, siba might be considered a veritable institution. It is siba that allows the tribes to take breath for a while, to try and re-establish their half-forgotten institutions, and to plunge once again into anarchy. But such revolts are generally without lasting effect, for, given the degree to which the local institutions have been broken down, it is no longer possible to reconstruct the republics as they were before. The only important effect that they have is to weaken the Empire itself, which has shown itself able, in the long run, to break down Berber society, but has never managed to organise it successfully.

Siba (that is to say, general revolt) breaks out whenever a Sultan dies and the price of gunpowder in the towns doubles as soon as his death is announced; or else, it develops when he has suffered some humiliating defeat somewhere in the Empire that disastrously reduces his prestige. At the same time, factions develop within the palace of the defunct or defeated Sultan. Frequently, pretenders to the throne have their younger brothers strangled, or, if they are out of each others' reach, they agree to join battle in order to gain control of their share of Morocco. The major periods of siba that have occurred during the last few reigns followed the deaths of Sidi Mohammed ben 'Abdullah (1790-1797), Moulay 'Abderrahman (1859-1864) and Moulay el Hassan (1894-1897).

The siba tended to be more violent if the country had experienced a long period of law and order—that is, of despotism. We are not talking here about the many local revolts by means of which the people would show their resentment of the yoke imposed upon them by the Makhzen, but of those periods when the revolutionary fervour would seize the whole country and instantly reduce the Bled el Makhzen to the towns and to tribes long since Arabised. As soon as news of the existence of siba in the neighbouring tribes was heard— and this sort of news spread like wildfire—the qāids would shut themselves in their qasbahs or, if caught on a journey, would find refuge in the qasbah of a friend. The tribesmen would gather, besiege the qasbah and destroy it, while the qāid, put to flight by the burning of his fortress, would seek refuge at the tomb of a marabout or else flee to the home of a neighbouring qāid who had managed to contain the revolt in his territory. The first act—after the general looting of the former qāid's possessions, each individual taking back what belonged to him—would be the reconstitution of the council of notables and the wholesale restoration of former Berber institutions.

The behaviour of the tribesmen requires careful examination at this point, for it could be said that there is no better way of judging the stage reached in the transformation of a region under Makhzen control than to look at the political system during siba. In the high mountains the Berber constitution would be completely restored; lower down, the council of the *ait arba'in* would be reformed, but it was no longer known how to appoint the moqaddem. Further down, in the foothills, where the new type of division had obliterated the boundaries of the cantons, the notables of the whole tribe, or the shaykhs, would form the council and govern as best they could, each one of them trying to build up his position so as to be in a position to become qāid when he felt that the period of siba was virtually at an end. Soon, in the plains and in the regions near the plains, cantons and tribes left to themselves would drift into the most dreadful anarchy. The apathy of chaos would then come to replace the enthusiasm of the early days; everywhere wars would break out between leffs and private feuds between rival families. Then, one day, the Sultan who had managed to defeat the other pretenders would appear once again in the region with his mehalla—his huge army composed of troops and contingents recruited from a variety of places. Their *ait arba'in* abandoned and betrayed, the tribesmen would take up the yoke again without too much regret.

The importance of these periods of revolt demonstrates the weakness of the central organisation of the Makhzen. We have shown how the organisation of the province controlled by a Makhzen qāid in Berber territory differs from that dominated by an amghar or a great lord, who are in power through their own political efforts. They can count on a loyal group, on the men of their own canton or tribe; the official qāid, on the other hand, has servants recruited from anywhere and who are often in fact strangers or slaves. The Sherifian Empire also seems to lack this central core, the support of loyal tribes, which are to be found at the heart of any strongly constituted Berber state. Its power is more diffuse, and more uncertain as well; it is based upon the towns, which are themselves isolated in Makhzen territory, and surrounded by poorly controlled, marauding and aggressive tribes. In short, the disintegration of Berber society under the Empire generates, in the end, an enormous growth of anarchy, that can be limited for a while by a strong Sultan, but which feeds dangerously on both generalised siba and local revolts. Under these conditions no prosperity, no progress even, can be achieved. It is this anarchy that brought about the downfall and ruin of independent Morocco.

The Berber Empires

In the Middle Ages however, there emerged infinitely more vigorous political systems than the Sherifian Makhzen (of Arab origin) based upon the traditions of Islam and of Arab civilisation.[2] It is important to examine these empires and kingdoms of Berber origin which succeeded one another in the Maghreb during the course of history, and which had a totally different structure.

The Fatimid Empire, the Almoravid and Almohad Empires, and

the Merinid Empire in its early stages, all belonged to this second type, which is characterised only by a greater degree of organisation than that of the small Berber states whose growth we studied in the south of Morocco, for its basis remains specifically Berber. In order really to understand the nature of these empires we must search in the often incomplete writings of the historians for accounts of how they were established, grew and disappeared. We shall limit ourselves here to a brief discussion of the morphology of two of them, the empires of the Fatimids and of the Almohads. Then we shall try, somewhat ambitiously perhaps, to compare them with the very incomplete shape of a state that a Berber leader has been forming before our very eyes during the past four years; we are referring to the Riffian state created by ʿAbd el Krim. We shall see from these three cases that the basic principles underlying the formation of the Berber kingdoms of the south of Morocco are still in operation today.

The extraordinary saga of the Fatimids, who in the tenth century took possession of Ifriqiya, Sicily, Egypt and Syria one after the other, is well known. It is explained very simply in terms of the construction from the inside outwards that characterises the Berber state. First of all we find the man claiming to be the Mehdi and his servant establishing themselves in the mountains inhabited by the Kutama tribes, and rallying these tribesmen around them by their stirring religious propaganda. Then, having made swift progress, thanks to their religious appeal, through those initial stages on the road to power which are always so difficult for a secular leader, they launched their followers into the conquest of the towns of Ifriqiya (modern Tunisia). Later, it was still the Kutama who conquered Egypt for them. And when they moved into Syria, they took the rest of these tribes with them. Each time they would reward the tribesmen with a military command, with slaves or with a sum of money. The Kutama were their Makhzen and their personal guard.

At the beginning, the Almohads proceeded in the same way, but they were able to create from the outset a more stable structure, and one which could support an empire for over a century. During the first years of the movement, a religious reformer was able fairly easily to establish his authority over a group of mountain tribes inhabiting areas of the Nefis valley, and he set up his base at Tinmel. But the body of fighting men of the Masmuda that Ibn Tumert gathered around him had other aims than to bring about a renaissance of the primitive purity of early Islam—they were more interested in the conquest of the rich lands of the plains under Almoravid control. One after the other the mountain tribes of Morocco were rallied to the cause by Ibn Tumert's Almohads, and were attached to one or other of the five privileged tribes by ties of adoption. Finally, they seized the plains, and the cities of Fes and Marrakesh, and soon took over Andalusia and the whole of the Maghreb.

But the five tribes of the early years continued to play a dominant role in the government of the Almohad state; they provided an Almohad nobility, ranked according to the assistance that each group had given to the cause of the Mehdi. A sixth tribe had to be added to the priviliged five: that of the Kumia, from the region of Nedromah (to the north of Tlemsen), from which the new head of state, 'Abd el Mumen, Ibn Tumert's successor, originally came. It was this Almohad central alliance which provided governors for the towns, military commanders for the various provinces, tax collectors and even preachers and officials to supervise commerce. The Council of the Almohads (a sort of aristocratic adaptation of the *ait arba'in* to the circumstances of an empire), remained close to the sovereign, intervening in times of crisis and during interregna. Later, discord spread through this body, and the rulers themselves came to fear these descendants of the warriors of Tinmel. On the other hand, the forces of the Masmuda were eventually to become too weak to maintain their grip on the enormous empire. The decline of the Almohad tribes marks also the decline of their powerful Makhzen. It would seem at the very least interesting to underline the importance of the role played by the Berber structure of the Almohad state in the formation and consolidation of the most magnificent empire the Maghreb had known since the fall of Rome.

It is a little curious to turn to the part played by 'Abd el Krim—the petty Riffian leader of a confederation of tribes—after having spoken of 'Abd el Mumen, master of all the Maghreb and also of Spain; but the first phases of 'Abd el Krim's brief episode bear certain similarities to the early days of the Almohad Empire during the period of its foundation in the heart of the western High Atlas.[3]

'Abd el Krim, son of a qadi in Ajdir, would have been unable to rise above the petty family quarrels—which are so bitter in the Rif that, as we have mentioned, each homestead is like a little isolated fortress—had unity not been created in the central Rif by the threat of Spanish incursions during the summer of 1921. The fervour of a holy war united the Riffians in a flash, and a strong force of thirty thousand men were soon on the march towards Alhucemas. A resounding victory, which was largely the result of the appalling organisation of the Spanish expeditionary forces, made 'Abd el Krim one of the most esteemed leaders in the pursuit of war and the sale of prisoners. Thanks to these exceptional circumstances he was able to clear, at one leap, the first two hurdles in the race for political power: the takeover of a canton and then of a tribe. The Beni Wariaghel—his fellow-tribesmen—provided him from the very first months with the loyal core needed to build a Berber state. In the two years that followed he rallied around him the tribes of the western Rif—the Boqqoia, Beni Itteft, Temsaman and Beni Tuzin—in somewhat the same way as Ibn Tumert gathered together the five tribes of the Nefis. These followers provided him with the forces with which he could impose his authority on the rest of the Rif. The Beni Wariaghel provided military commanders and governors—who were given the title of 'pasha'—for positions created in the territories of conquered tribes.

In 1924 he managed to gain control of the Jbala and then began to build up the personnel for a small but modern administration. Those who were given the pretentious title of 'minister'—pretentious if one thinks of the usual anarchy of Riffian society—were 'Abd el Krim's childhood companions and sons of the *ait arba'in* from his own village, while other members of the original tribes were given commands in far-off areas. Meanwhile 'Abd el Krim continued his efforts to unify the whole region, eliminating the small local leaders, confining the marabouts to their houses, and suppressing customary law. Swept on by his own ambitions and by that even greater force —the internal dynamic of a Berber state in a period of growth— 'Abd el Krim soon turned his attention to the conquest of the tribes subdued by the French, and in 1925 war broke out all along the frontier of our 'zone'.

One year later, 'Abd el Krim was defeated after a few days' fighting—so short a time that his downfall mystified everyone. The secret of his failure is simple: his own tribe, the Beni Wariaghel, who constituted the central core of his Riffian state, was attacked by French and Spanish forces. At a stroke, the entire political structure crumbled, and 'Abd el Krim was left alone, with only those that he called his 'Makhzen'—the sons of his own village *ait arba'in*— remaining with him. He had no other choice then than to entrust himself to the generosity of the French in order to avoid complete destruction. This he did, coming of his own accord to give himself up to the general in command of our troops and asking for protection for his family and his companions.

In this series of events we can discern the operation of all the principles which determine the 'Berber policy,' adopted by political leaders. These last events of recent years can easily be classified with those of earlier historical periods.

Weakness and Strength of Berber Society

Having come to the end of this analysis of political organisation among the Berber tribes of Morocco, it could hardly be claimed that we have now reached that final point from which one may obtain a vision of the full sweep of history. The fact is that, in the case of Berber society, everything remains a little dull, monotonous and without much relief, despite the consideration that one can give to human affairs. However one strives to rise above the crude facts, one never manages to produce those great and brilliant historical landscapes that Renan describes so well for the Middle East, when he lays before us, as if from the peak of a high mountain, the great currents of civilisation sweeping in from every possible direction to provide a rich landscape. On the contrary, most often one can perceive nothing but a tangled network of dry ravines, and a desert of worthless happenings which deaden the spirit and which appear to defy all logical classification.

We have attempted, in this study of Berber institutions, to give a little order to the chaos that North African history often appears to be. We know how the great historian, Ibn Khaldun, struck by the apparent disorder of social life in this country, broken only by the brief emergence and decline of the Berber dynasties, sought to find the explanation for these alternating phases of conquest and decadence. He suggested (as we have seen) that the cause lies in the way in which the luxurious life of the cities currupts and weakens the formerly rough and vigorous inhabitants of the wide open spaces who, although they are really quite capable of seizing power, nevertheless remain incapable of resisting the slow softening that accompanies the settled life. For him, urban civilisation and the creative power of the empire builders represent two rival and antithetical forces which ceaselessly destroy each other in turn. And, being a true Oriental, filled with resignation before the divine will, Ibn Khaldun concluded that there is no permanence but in Allah.

Perhaps we can go further than this in the search for the fundamental causes. The analysis that we have given of the political organisation of Berber tribes—that of 'ordered anarchy', which is in keeping with the spirit of this race—explains well enough the apathy

I

and stagnation into which the Maghreb tended to sink. When vigorous and ambitious leaders raised themselves up above their brothers the 'concentric' structure of their little states helps us to understand the speed with which they manage to build them up. As for their sudden decline, it was due less to the softening of city life than to a more general phenomenon—the erosion of that central core of strength which is the heart of the Berber state. Sometimes this erosion is brought about by the dispersal of those loyal troops throughout a vast empire, as happened with the Almohads; sometimes by their mingling with numerous foreign elements—a sort of dilution—such as probably occurred in the case of the Merinid tribes, surrounded as they were by Zeneta and Arabs. In yet other cases, it is brought about by a military defeat, as we saw four years ago in the case of the little Riffian state forged by 'Abd el Krim. A simpler cause is the existence of cleavages between members of the leader's own family within the mountain Berber political system at the same time as revolt is brewing among the subject groups.

As for the feebleness of the Arab states, like those of the Sa'dians and Filalians in Morocco, this is the result of the impotence of a central government sapped by the fever of siba and of tribal revolts. The Sherifian Makhzen knew very well how to destroy Berber society, but it had no idea of how to use the pieces to build something greater. And this patchwork of former states constituted by the subject tribes reveals itself, when tried, to be a poor material from which to construct a Muslim state. A system foreign to the oriental world is required if a lasting empire is to be built in the Maghreb— one like that of Rome, or else like the one that we brought to Algiers a century ago with the fleet of Charles the Tenth, when we arrived in North Africa.

NOTES

1   The major features of the Moroccan state in pre-colonial times are analysed in many works, from several different points of view. See, for example, Abun-Nasr's *A History of the Maghrib*; Burke's 'The Image of the Moroccan State in French Historical Literature . . .'; Gellner's *Saints of the Atlas* and his article on 'Tribalism and social change in North Africa' in *French-Speaking Africa: the search for Identity*, edited by W. H. Lewis; Yves Lacoste's *Ibn Khaldun . . .*, Chapter 1; Lahbabi's *Le Gouvernement Marocain à l'Aube du XXe Siècle*; and Waterbury's *The Commander of the Faithful*, Chapter 1.

2   In this chapter we find the dichotomies: 'Arab'–'Berber'; 'Makhzen'– 'Siba' (or tribal political systems); and *shari'a* (Islamic religious law)—*'urf* (Berber customary law) brought into alignment with each other. The antagonism between Makhzen and Siba is characterised also as an opposition between Islamic religious law and tribal customary law and 'law and order' is contrasted

with the concept of 'justice'. It is suggested that the destruction of Berber society by the essentially 'Arab' Makhzen resulted only in the establishment of a weak and internally conflict-ridden state; it is then suggested that this primarily *internal* situation brought about the downfall and ruin of independent Morocco. No mention is made of the effect that Morocco's increasing involvement throughout the nineteenth century (and even before) in the European-dominated international economy had on the internal situation.

3 An extremely detailed analysis of the origins and development of the 'Ripublik' in the Rif is given in Chapters XV and XVI of David Hart's forthcoming study of the Ait Wariaghel of the central Rif. He refers there to the concept, utilised by J. A. Barnes in his *Politics in a Changing Society* of a 'snowball' effect in the growth of a state.

Conclusion

Berber society, through its inability to construct lasting states and through the inertia with which it confronts those who would found new states within it, retains within itself an infinite capacity to endure. It accepts outwardly those forms of civilisation which come from the outside: Rome and Christianity, Arabia and Islam and now, in the twentieth century, France. But it never gives more than a part of itself and keeps for itself its secret essence. Its local dialects preserve an entire inner existence which is expressed in its poor literature, but which shelters, nevertheless, esoteric and enduring beliefs. Above all it maintains something that we cannot call 'individualism', but rather a 'particularism' of tribe and village. It preserves in its core the nostalgic and ever-faithful memory of the period of canton independence, and of leff solidarity, while at the same time the attachment to the patriarchal family remains so strong that it is still intact wherever one looks, even after so many centuries of Islamic penetration and after so many decades of French influence.

What will happen in the future to Berber society; that is to say, to the secret soul of this ancient land which gave itself to Islam without wishing to assimilate entirely, in the social and political sphere, the whole system of Arab colonialism, and which still defends jealously its several thousand years' old heritage of customs, beliefs and traditions? One would need to be both a prophet and omniscient to be able to outline the evolution of whole peoples with a sure hand. It is, however, possible to identify a few 'constants' and to construct a few hypotheses. It is certain that Berber society, having undergone the influence of the religion of the Prophet and its language for many centuries, will remain faithful to this revered past; also the general tendencies of Berber society are unlikely to diverge noticeably from those of other Muslim countries of Africa and the Middle East. It is extremely difficult to believe, however, that there could develop among the Berbers states drawing upon their own national heritage and literature, linking up again with the distant traditions of a pre-Islamic past, as developed in Turkey, Iran and Afghanistan. The Berber heritage is too poor to lend itself to such a renaissance. Whatever the circumstances of political development in North Africa, this possibility can be discounted. Is that to say, as is perhaps too widely supposed, that Berber society is now destroyed and that the Maghreb will become, once again, a province of the ancient historic empire of the Middle East that was founded in the early centuries by the Omayyads, the Abbassids and the Fatimids, and more recently reconstituted under the Turks? This would be to forget that the best preserved Berber provinces in the Maghreb—those in which tribal vitality was the strongest—have retained a more or less complete autonomy with regard to the conquerors of the Middle East.

Is it not wiser to believe that a day will come when the Berber peoples of North Africa, called to the light by the attainment of modern learning, will finally emerge from their obscure villages to play their role as citizens, *en masse*? Taking their place within true States they will become aware, for the first time, of the deep qualities and aspirations of their race in such a way that, as they gradually construct African nations, they will give these a new originality which will prove a sort of revelation for history. Perhaps there will appear among them great men who will leave the print of their genius upon all their actions. A race which has produced a Saint Augustin in the spiritual domain and an 'Abd el Mumen in the political has sufficiently demonstrated the wealth of its resources. Shall we see modern Berber society emerge from its obscurity to give birth to new African Muslim nations, owing allegiance at the same time to Islam and to the West?

Many Frenchmen have thought, for over a century, that it would be easy to assimilate the Berbers, because they were not Arabs; many Arabs have, for twenty years at least, proclaimed the Berbers as their racial brothers, their comrades-in-arms in the struggle against the West because they were Muslims. It is possible that history will prove both these sets of beliefs wrong by producing in North Africa a hybrid political variety: Muslim communities, yet strongly western-ised, seeking to achieve a synthesis of the different influences, and placing themselves between civilisations, in an intermediary position, just as they are situated geographically on the shores of the Mediter-ranean at the interface between Europe and Africa. But for such a development to take place it is necessary, above all, for the old conservative Berber society, as we have described it here, to begin to wither away.

That is, in fact, what is happening, although more slowly than one might imagine, for its ability to preserve and to retain appear infinite. That is why, before thinking of its future, it is first of all essential to understand fully its past, which survives before our eyes.

A Glossary of Arabic and Berber Words

agadir   term employed in various parts of the Suss for the collective storehouse in which 'patriarchal families' (lineages) store their grain.

agellid   King, monarch.

ait arba'in   literally: the house of the forty. The term refers to the council of elders at the tribal level the number of whose members in fact varies considerably.

'alam   literally: a flag, or emblem. In the context here it is used to refer to an identifiable political association or coalition.

amghar   a political leader by virtue of his recognition or his election as such by his own community. Thus he differs from the *qāid* who has a piece of paper issued by the central government confirming his authority. Montagne's analysis is concerned more with the self-made leader than with the elected leader, but he discusses the way in which election as *amin* may enable a man to become an *amghar*.

amin   the president of the council of elders, or, more loosely, an administrator.

anflus   singular of *inflas*.

arsh   the term used in Kabylia for what Montagne calls a canton.

'ashur   tithe.

baraka   sanctity, divine blessing, the power to bless. An attribute of holy men and saints (marabouts). *Shorfa* have *baraka* by virtue of their descent from the Prophet.

gela'a   the term employed by the transhumants of the Aures in Algeria for the collective storehouse.

gish   the tax-exempt tribes of the *bled el makhzen* who provide the majority of the regular troops for the royal army, and who are allocated land by the Sultan in return for services done and services due.

ghorfa   the term employed in southern Tunisia for the collective storehouse.

hajib   chamberlain.

igherm   the term used by the pastoralists of the Central Atlas for the collective storehouse.

inflas   the elders in council, usually at the level of the canton, but also used to refer to the tribal council.

jama'a   a group of notables; the canton or even tribal council of elders.

jebel   a mountain or hill.

kharaj   a tax collected from infidels or foreigners. Also a tax collected in the early years after the Hejira from new converts to Islam who were left in possession of their lands.

khums   literally: a fifth. Here either a fraction of the tribe or a tribal segment.

leff   a political alliance or coalition, members of which may come to each others' assistance in offence or in defence against members of other leffs (*elfuf*).

makhzen   literally: treasury, the central government. Used to refer to all sections of the central administration and bureaucracy and of local and regional administration also.

mbarkin   the fortunate or blessed ones; see *baraka*.

mehalla   a military column belonging to the forces of the *makhzen* (generally), or a military expedition.

mia   literally: a hundred. A group of a hundred individuals, households, or whatever.

moqaddem   literally: the one in charge or the one appointed. A leader or the president of the council of elders elected by the other notables.

msakhrin   a messenger.

qadi   a religious judge applying and working within the framework of the Qur'anic law.

qāid   an official appointed by the Sultan to act as the local official of the *makhzen*, administering a tribe or group of tribes. Occasionally it refers loosely to a self-made political leader among the tribes.

qanun   civil or secular (i.e. non-Qur'anic) law.

qasbah   a fortress of any kind; often a fortified storehouse.

rba'   literally: a quarter, or a fourth. Here either a fraction of the tribe or a tribal segment.

ribat   a pledge or pact.

sherif   a holy man by virtue of descent from the Prophet.
  (pl. *shorfa*)

shaykh   a minor official appointed by the makhzen to administer a tribe or tribal segment under the authority of the *qāid*. Sometimes it refers to a minor political leader.

siba   translated variously as dissidence, insolence, rebellion, anarchy, the term generally refers to the areas and sectors of society (usually the tribes) outside the direct control of the *makhzen*.

sokhta   a curse of particular potency.

soff   a political alliance or coalition; see *leff*. The term is used by Montagne to refer to political cleavages and alignments among the Kabyles of Algeria. The word is a corruption of the Arabic *saff*, meaning a class, line of troops, etc.

taqbilt   tribe or tribal segment. From the Arabic *qabila*, usually translated as: a tribe.

tighermt   feminine or diminutive form of *igherm*.

tuiza   a form of cooperative and communal work-force. Either voluntary and reciprocal or else used as a corvée by the notables or by the *amghar*.

ukil   a lawyer, or an agent, official.

umana   plural of *amin*.

'urf   customary tribal law.

zawia   the centre of a religious brotherhood, or of a holy lineage of saints (marabouts). Also used to refer to the social organisation of the lodge or religious centre.

zekkat   religious tithe or tax redistributed to the poor and needy.

Bibliography

Abun-Nasr, J., 'The Salafiyya Movement in Morocco: the Religious Bases of the Moroccan Nationalist Movement', St. Antony's Papers No. 16, *Middle Eastern Affairs*, No. 3, London, 1963.

Abun-Nasr, J., *A History of the Maghrib*, Cambridge University Press, London, 1965.

Apthorpe, R., *People Planning and Development Studies*, Frank Cass & Co., 1971.

Aron, R., *Main Currents in Sociological Thought*, Weidenfeld & Nicolson, London, London, 1970.

Asad, T., 'Market model, Class Structure and Consent: a Reconsideration of Swat Political Organisation, *Man (NS)*, Vol. 7, No. 1.

Bailey, F. G., *Stratagems and Spoils*, Blackwells, Oxford, 1969.

Balandier, G., *Political Anthropology*, Penguin, London, 1970.

Barnes, J. A., *Politics in a Changing Society*, Manchester University Press, Manchester, 1969.

Barth, F., 'Segmentary Opposition and the Theory of Games: a Study of Pathan Organisation, *Journal of the Royal Anthropological Institute*, Vol. 89, Pt. 1.

Barth, F., *Political Leadership among Swat Pathans*, LSE Monograph Series No. 19, Athlone Press, London, 1959.

Benet, F., 'Explosive Markets: the Berber Highlands', in Polanyi, Arensberg and Pearson (eds), *Trade and Markets in Early Empires*, The Free Press, Chicago, 1957.

Bloch, M., *Feudal Society*, Routledge & Kegan Paul, London, 1961.

Bohannan, L., 'A Genealogical Charter', *Africa*, 1952.

Bottomore, T. B., *Sociology: a Guide to Problems and Literature*, George Allen & Unwin, London, 1971.

Brignon, J. *et al.*, *Histoire du Maroc*, Casablanca, 1967.

Burke, E., 'The Image of the Moroccan State in French Historical Literature: New Light on the Origins of Lyautey's Berber Policy', in Gellner and Micaud (eds), *Arabs and Berbers*, Duckworth, London, 1972.

Cochrane, G., *Development Anthropology*, Oxford University Press, New York, 1971.

Cohen, A., 'Political Anthropology: the Analysis of the Symbolism of Power Relations,' *Man (NS)*, Vol. 4, No. 2.

Cour, A., *Etablissement des Dynasties des Chorfa au Maroc*, Paris.

Dawood, N. J., *see* Ibn Khaldun.

Doutté, E., 'Une Mission d'Etudes', *Renseignements Coloniaux*, 1901.

Doutté, E., *Organisation Sociale et Domestique des Haha*, Bulletin de l'Afrique Française, Renseignements Coloniaux, 1905.

Doutté, E., *Marrakech*, Paris, 1905.

Doutté, E., *Missions au Maroc, En Tribu*, Paul Geuthner, Paris, 1914.

Durkheim, E., *The Rules of the Sociological Method* (originally published in 1895), Free Press, New York, 1938.

Durkheim, E., *The Division of Labor in Society* (originally published in 1893). Free Press, New York, 1968.

Engels, F., *The Origin of the Family, Private Property and the State*. (Originally published in 1884), Foreign Languages Publishing House, Moscow, 1954.

Evans-Pritchard, E. E., *The Nuer*, Oxford University Press, Oxford, 1940.

Evans-Pritchard, E. E., *The Sanusi of Cyrenaica*, Oxford University Press, London, 1949.

Firth, R., *Essays on Social Organization and Values*, Athlone Press, London, 1964.

Fogg, W., 'The Suq: A Study in the Human Geography of Morocco', *Geography*, Vol. 17.

Fogg, W., 'Villages and Suqs in the High Atlas Mountains of Morocco', *Scottish Geographical Magazine*, Vol. 51, No. 3.

Fogg, W., 'The Importance of Tribal Markets in the Commercial Life of the Countryside of North West Morocco', *Africa*, Vol. XII, No. 4.

Forde, D., 'Applied Anthropology in Government: British Africa', in Kroeber, (ed), *Anthropology Today*, University of Chicago Press, Chicago, 1953.

Fortes, M., & Evans-Pritchard, E. E. (eds), *African Political Systems*, Oxford University Press, London, 1961 (originally published in 1940).

Foster, G. M., *Applied Anthropology*, Little-Brown & Co., Boston, 1969.

Fox, R., *Kinship and Marriage*, Penguin Books, London, 1968.

Gellner, E. A., 'Tribalism and Social Change in North Africa', in Hewis (ed), *French-speaking Africa: the Search for Identity*, New York, 1965.

Gellner, E. A., *Saints of the Atlas*, Weidenfeld & Nicolson, London, 1969.

Gellner, E. A. & Micaud, C. (eds), *Arabs and Berbers*, Duckworth, London, 1972.

Godelier, M., 'La notion de 'mode de production asiatique' et les schémas marxistes d'évolution des sociétés' in *Sur le Mode de Production Asiatique*, CERM, Paris, 1969.

Godelier, M. (ed), *Sur les Sociétés Précapitalistes*, CERM, Paris, 1970.

Haddon, A. C., 'Presidential Address: Anthropology, its Position and Needs', *Journal of the Anthropological Institute*, Vol. 33.

Halstead, J. P., *Rebirth of a Nation: the Origins and Rise of Moroccan Nationalism*, Harvard Middle Eastern Monograph Series, XVIII, Harvard University Press, Cambridge, Mass., 1967.

Hanoteau, L. A. & Letourneux, A. *La Kabylie et les Coutumes Kabyles*, Paris, 1893.

Harris, M., *The Rise of Anthropological Theory*, Routledge & Kegan Paul, London, 1968.

Hart, D. M., 'An Ethnographic Survey of the Riffian Tribe of Aith Waryaghil', *Tamuda*, II, 1.

Hart, D. M., 'Segmentary Systems and the Role of the "Five Fifths" in Tribal Morocco', *Revue de l'Occident Musulman et de la Mediterrannée* No. 3, 1er trimestre, 1967.

Khaldun, Ibn, *The Muqaddimah: an Introduction to History*, (ed) N. J. Dawood, Bollingen Series, Princeton University Press, Princeton, 1969.

Krader, L., *Formation of the State*, Prentice Hall Inc., New Jersey, 1968.

Lacoste, Y., *Ibn Khaldun: naissance de l'histoire passé du tiers monde*, Maspero, Paris, 1969.

Lahbabi, M., *Le Gouvernement Marocain à l'Aube du XXe Siècle*, E.T.N.A., Rabat, 1958.

Leach, E. R., *Political Systems of Highland Burma*, Beacon Press, Boston, 1965 (originally published 1954).

Lowie, R. H., *The Origin of the State*, Russell, New York, 1961.

Macalister, A., 'Presidential Address', *Journal of the Anthropological Institute*, Vol. 24.

Mair, L. P., 'The Social Sciences in Africa South of the Sahara: the British Contribution', *Human Organization*, Vol. 19.

Maquet, J., 'Objectivity in Anthropology', *Current Anthropology*, Vol. 5, No. 1.

Masqueray, E., *La Formation des Cités chez les Populations Sédentaires de l'Algérie*, Laval, Paris, 1866.

Maurois, A., *Marshal Lyautey*, John Lane, The Bodley Head, London, 1931.

Maxwell, G., *Lords of the Atlas: the Rise and Fall of the House of Glaoua, 1893-1956*, Pan Books, London, 1970.

Meillassoux, C., 'From Reproduction to Production: a Marxist approach to Economic Anthropology', *Economy and Society*, Vol. 1, No. 1, 1972.

Meillet, A. & Cohen, M., *Les Langues du Monde*, Champion, Paris, 1924.

Miege, J. L., *Le Maroc et l'Europe*, Presses Universitaires de France, Paris, 1961-3.

Mikesell, M. W., 'The Role of Tribal Markets in Morocco', *Geographical Review*, XLVIII, October.

Montagne, R., *Les Berbères et le Makhzen dans le Sud du Maroc: essai sur la transformation politique des Berbères sédentaires (groupe chleuh)*, Felix Alcan, Paris, 1930.

Montagne, R., *La Vie Sociale et la Vie Politique des Berbères*, Afrique Française, Paris, 1931.

Montagne, R., *La Civilisation du Désert: nomades d'Orient et d'Afrique*, Paris, 1947.

Montagne, R., *Naissance du Prolétariat Marocain*, Paris, 1951.

Montagne, R., *Révolution au Maroc*, Paris, 1953.

Morgan, L. H., *Ancient Society*, World Publishing, New York, 1877.

Peters, E. L., 'Some structural aspects of the feud among the camel-herding Bedouin of Cyrenaica', *Africa*, XXXVII.

Radcliffe-Brown, A. R., 'The Methods of Ethnology and Social Anthropology', *South African Journal of Science*, Vol. 20.

Radcliffe-Brown, A. R., *Structure and Function in Primitive Societies*, Cohen and West, London, 1952.

Scham, A., *Lyautey in Morocco; Protectorate Administration, 1912-1925*, University of California Press, Berkeley, 1970.

Shinar, P., 'Abd al-Qadar and Abd al-Krim: Religious Influences on their Thought and Action', *Asian and African Studies*, 1.

Simon, H., 'Les études berbères au Maroc et leurs applications en matière de politique et de l'administration', *Archives Berbères*, I, 1915.

Stauder, J., 'The Function of Functionalism: the Adaptation of British Social Anthropology to British Colonialism in Africa', paper presented to the Meetings of the American Anthropological Association, November 1971.

Waterbury, J., *The Commander of the Faithful: the Moroccan Political Elite—a Study in Segmented Politics*, Weidenfeld & Nicolson, London, 1970.

Westermarck, E., *Ritual and Belief in Morocco*, London, 1926.

Woolman, D. S., *Rebels in the Rif: Abd al Krim and the Rif rebellion*, Oxford University Press, London, 1969.

Yacono, X., *Les Bureaux Arabes et l'évolution des genres de vie indigènes dans l'ouest du Tell algérois*, Larose, Paris, 1953.